MOON NODE ASTROLOGY

MOON NODE ASTROLOGY

The Inner Compass of Evolution

Bruno & Louise Huber

HopeWell
Knutsford, England

Originally published in German entitled 'Mondknoten Astrologie'
by Bruno & Louise Huber
Copyright © 1991 API-Verlag, Adliswil/ Zürich (Switzerland)

First published in English in 1995 by Samuel Weiser, Inc.

This edition published 2005 by HopeWell

HopeWell,
PO Box 118, Knutsford
Cheshire WA16 8TG, U.K.

Translated by Transcript, Ltd., Wales.

Jacket: adapted from original by Bruno Huber

ISBN 0-9547680-3-5

Warmest thanks to all the friends who interest themselves in Astrological Psychology and support our work. We also thank our collaborators for their active help in the preparation of this book:

Udo Bender
Ilse Conrad
Daniel Cuny
Lotti Ehrat
Elke Gut
Michael-A. Huber
Ursula Hunkeler
Johanna Kohler
Wolfhard König
John Portmann
Rita Schafroth
Werner Stephan
Dr. Monika von Torne-Linder

And to all those who have waited so long for this book, we should like to express our gratitude for your patience.

Space is an entity in which many worlds of time and space can come into existence and vanish—next to or following one another.

—Bruno Huber

Contents

Part 1: Structure and Function
of Moon-Node Astrology
by Bruno Huber

Part 2: The Moon's Nodes and Esotericism
by Louise Huber

List of Illustrations

List of Charts

Astrological Psychology Institute (UK)

in association with Bruno and Louise Huber
Astologisch-Psychologisches Institut, Switzerland
Correspondence courses and workshops in Astrology,
Astrological Psychology and Counseling.

Full details of courses and workshop programs are included in API(UK)'s comprehensive prospectus. If you would like to receive a copy of this please contact:

Astrological Psychology Institute (UK)
PO Box 29, Upton, Wirral CH49 3BG, England
Tel: 00 44 (0)151 605 0039
Email: api.enquiries@btopenworld.com

There is also an associated service for printing Huber-style charts and chart data:

Richard Llewellyn, API(UK) Chart Data Service
PO Box 29, Upton, Wirral CH49 3BG, England
Tel: 00 44 (0)151 606 8551
Email: r.llewellyn@btinternet.com

Software for generating Huber-style charts, including the Moon Node Chart, can be obtained from:

Elly Gibbs
Tel: 00 44 (0)151 605 0039
Email: software.api@btinternet.com

or on the internet from:
www.catharsoftware.com

Books and API(UK) publications related to the Huber Method can be obtained from:

Linda Tinsley, API(UK) Bookshop
70 Kensington Road, Southport PR9 0RY, UK
Tel: 00 44 (0)1704 544652
Email: Lucindatinsley@tiscali.co.uk

Note to the Reader

This book is for "New Age" readers who are asking the old question, "Quo Vadis?" and are looking to astrology for answers to some of the deeper problems concerning esoteric relationships, spiritual development, and the meaning of life. Such questions can indeed be answered if we extend the usual astrological procedures to the Moon's Nodes, the Moon-Node axis, and the Moon-Node horoscope. The present book describes this new method, which we call Moon-Node Astrology.

In Part 1 will be found everything necessary to know about astronomical patterns, and about the psychological meaning, structure, and function of the Moon's Nodes. Part 1 has been prepared from tapes of seminars held for the last ten years. Part 2 has been written in response to the increasing interest in esoteric matters, and examines the Moon-Node horoscope in the light of evolution and incarnation. There is helpful advice on making a judgment; and three charts have been taken from our casebooks to illustrate counseling techniques. The latter feature has been included in response to a wish frequently expressed by professional astrologers and therapists, and by many students of astrological psychology.

We hope that the book will go a long way toward demonstrating the universality of astrology, and that it will promote holistic thinking in practitioners of the arts.

—Bruno and Louise Huber
Adliswil, July 1991

Abbreviations

AC	=	Ascendant	HC	= House Cusps
IC	=	Imum Coeli	LP	= Low Point
DC	=	Descendent	IP	= Invert Point
MC	=	Medium Coeli	BH	= Birth Horoscope
AP	=	Age Point	HH	= House Horoscope
TAP	=	Temperament Age Point	MNH	= Moon-Node Horoscope

Symbols of the Planets

Sun	☉	♂	Mars
Moon	☾	♃	Jupiter
Saturn	♄	♅	Uranus
Mercury	☿	♆	Neptune
Venus	♀	♇	Pluto
North Node	☊		

Symbols of the Signs

Aries	♈	♎	Libra
Taurus	♉	♏	Scorpio
Gemini	♊	♐	Sagittarius
Cancer	♋	♑	Capricorn
Leo	♌	♒	Aquarius
Virgo	♍	♓	Pisces

Introduction

Moon-Node astrology owes its existence to many years of research in response to the need for a holistic view of the horoscope. It supplies the answers to questions which have troubled humanity time and again—questions concerning the meaning of existence. As is well known, the methods used have to suit the way in which questions are formulated. This fundamental scientific rule applies to astrological research, too. It is clear that questions concerned with the solution to psychological and entirely general spiritual problems cannot be tackled in the same fashion as questions about outward happiness and material prosperity.

Nowadays, more and more people are studying astrology because they cannot make satisfactory sense of their daily lives on the basis of what they have learned at school or in their professions. They hope that astrological knowledge will expand their horizons and release them from external and internal constraints. In fact, this preoccupation with astrology has brought about an increased awareness and has helped many to think more freely. Now, Moon-Node astrology, in particular, provides a conceptual model by which each of us can measure, and gain a better understanding of, his or her existence. It makes insights possible into existential and predetermined conditionalities, and introduces synthesis and clarity into our synopses. It helps us, step-by-step, to overcome the fear-desire polarity and encourages the power of positive growth. It provides a means of understanding the unity and interplay of above and below, of inner and outer, of microcosm and macrocosm, and teaches us to see the various areas of life superordinated within a cosmic frame.

What is more, work on the Moon-Node horoscope gives fresh, esoteric, insights into the phenomenon of time. Tracing the long ages of human development, and realizing their meaning and purpose, alters our historical perspective. The thought that, collectively, we humans still have an immensely long period of time left to us for development is very comforting. And acceptance of the idea that individuals possess immortal souls, which have already shared in the development of mankind in the course of many incarnations and will participate in its future evolution, can save us from being caught up in today's "rat race." It enables us to resolve previously intractable problems, and to look at them objectively without magnifying them. Moon-Node astrology exemplifies the law of inclusion, the law of love, or the modern "both-and" type of thinking. It gives familiarity with laws governing development in time and space; and we are freed from the "either-or" logic of the past, which separated integral parts from one another. Holistic thinking combines conformity with cosmic law with respect for details.

A study of the Moon's Nodes is yet another feature of esoteric astrology, which involves a grand view of the universe—including everything and omitting nothing. There will always be room for exploration in such a comprehensive field of knowledge. In future, astrology will have to be based on universal laws in order to present a holistic picture of nature, humanity, the world, and the universe. For, when all is said and done, it remains the "ABC" of the cosmos—a key that opens the door to all-embracing and limitless knowledge.

Once its symbolism and rules of interpretation have been grasped, astrology will reveal wide-ranging connections that relate the world of human beings to dimensions far beyond everyday consciousness. Esoteric astrology comes closer than other cognitive methods to the fundamental principle of all that exists. It asks the central philosophical question concerning what ultimately holds the world together, and supplies answers that satisfy more than the intellect. Thus it rises above mere fortune-telling.

The need to realize how human life is woven into the cosmic Whole has come very much to the fore in recent decades. A new type of holistic chart interpretation has been gaining popularity as an alternative to the usual horoscope reading with its string of predictions. People today are much more interested in esoterism, and many study astrology just to learn what they can about their spiritual and psychological development. They want to know their karma and the purpose of their present incarnation. They strive for inner growth and to rid themselves of false ideas and behavior patterns. They make sacrifices, and undergo purifying experiences, crises, and transformations, in order to find reality; and it is there that Moon-Node astrology can be so helpful. Obviously, for a holistic chart interpretation made from the point of view of depth psychology, methods of integration must be discovered for convincing answers to the questions, "Who am I?" "From where have I come?" "Where am I going?"

The astrology of the past was concerned with externals, and followed a set of rules that could be combined to show good and bad trends. Modern astrology, on the other hand, looks into whys and wherefores, and is oriented toward living reality; it adopts principles that reflect organic, inner values. Such an astrology appeals to mature individuals who think for themselves and go their own way, and enables them—through increasing self-knowledge—to recognize the causes of faulty modes of behavior and to avoid or recover from mistakes. By comparing the Moon-Node horoscope with the natal chart, we can discover the deeper meaning of "blows of fate" and find out what learning process awaits us. This knowledge gives us a better understanding of others, too, and may even put it in our power to rescue them from desperate situations.

Reference to the Moon-Node horoscope makes possible a synthesis, or work of integration, both for the client and for the therapist and consultant. For example, during therapy, the shadow is relatively easy to uncover when the Moon-Node horoscope is used. Work on the shadow is an up-to-date and essential therapeutic task. Processes that take a long time with the employment of purely psychological methods, are positively reinforced, and are set in motion with much less effort. By studying the Moon-Node horoscope, the trained adviser and open-minded therapist (if experienced in the use of astrology during analysis) can exhibit spiritual connections, reveal deeper roots, and examine questions raised in connection with the laws of evolution, human karma, reincarnation, the meaning of life, and further growth.

During many years of teaching and consultancy work, we have been told by numerous students of astrology how fruitful they have found an understanding of the Nodes and of the Moon-Node horoscope. They were enabled to accept themselves for what they were, and could quickly deepen consciousness. Those with esoteric leanings recognized the roots of their problems in former lives; and many things in their present lives that they had been unable to accept made sense at last, being seen as part of a greater whole. They confirmed that, in this way, striking expansions of consciousness, transformations, and processes of self-development were unleashed, and that these were much more profound than mere character analysis of personality traits with their strengths and weaknesses.

Part 1

THE STRUCTURE
AND FUNCTION OF
MOON-NODE ASTROLOGY

by
Bruno Huber

Edited by Ilse Conrad, Dipl. API

Chapter 1

The Function
of the Moon's Nodes

The Moon as our Night Side • The Nodes: Dragon's Head and
Dragon's Tail • Stonehenge—the First Lunar Calendar • The
Moon-Node Axis as a Line of Development • Lode-stars of the
Psyche • The Ascending Node • The Descending Node • The
Rhythm of the Moon's Nodes • The Moon's Node and the
Ascendant • Exercise on the Moon's Node • Its Relationship
to the Ascendant • Example • The Moon's Node as an
Ameliorating Element •

The Moon as our Night Side

The Moon is one of the two lights that shine by day and by
night. The Moon illuminates the night. In a psychological
sense, too, it represents the night side of our psyche—the
ominous, the dark, and the unaccountable; whatever is not immediately evident, the shadow side. However, in this context, the
word shadow does not signify anything negative, but refers to values that lie hidden.

The contents of the shadow are not always accessible to waking
consciousness, but are more likely to be experienced in dreams.
Now, our dream-life, which lurks in the unconscious, has often
been likened to the Moon. Actually, except in the few days when it
is full, the Moon has a bright and a dark side. And we can say that
we have our own dark side, if we mean by "dark" not something
ghastly, but something unknown, hard to get at, and not standing
in the light.

Figure 1. The Dragon's Head and Dragon's Tail.

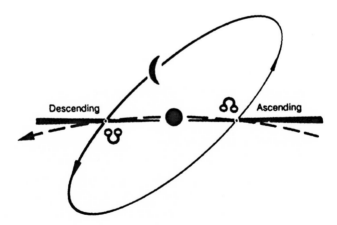

Figure 2. The Moon's path and the nodal axis.

What is more, the Moon is dual and divalent in certain respects: many things present themselves in the moonlight as polarities which, at times, seem to be mutually exclusive. There is no grayness to tone down their black and white. The Moon is the seat of this human tendency to paint stark contrasts—a tendency that obviously puts a strain on social relationships.

The Moon is our emotional "I," or means of making perceptual contact with the need to be loved. With our emotional "I," we probe the environment and sort it into pleasant and unpleasant, into white and black, into good and bad. Now, if we take a liking to someone and regard them as good, we feel let down when we discover their faults and failings in the course of living with them.

Thus, the emotional world of the Moon in us is a site of great illusions. All our memories are embedded in it. It houses a large amount of the past. These things are contained in its dark side, out of reach of our waking consciousness.

The Nodes—Dragon's Head and Dragon's Tail

From our particular observation post, the Sun appears to move around the Earth annually in a circular orbit. Its orbit lies in a plane known as the ecliptic. The Moon's orbit, like those of the planets, is almost in the same plane; but not quite. In fact, the plane of the Moon's orbit lies at an angle of 5 degrees to the ecliptic. When projected on the backcloth of the fixed stars, the paths of the Sun (the ecliptic) and the Moon seem to intersect at two points facing each other across the zodiac. These points of intersection are called the Moon's Nodes. See figure 1.

During its circuit round the earth in 28 days, the Moon crosses the path of the Sun once from south to north. This point of intersection is termed the Ascending Node. Fourteen days later, the Moon crosses the path of the Sun from north to south, and this point of intersection is termed the Descending Node (see figure 2). However, the Nodes do not remain where they are, but are continually being displaced in an east-west direction, i.e., they have a retrograde motion in the zodiac. The motion amounts to 1-1/2 degrees per month, and the Nodes complete their circuit of the zodiac in 18.6 years. This is relatively slow when compared with the periods of the planets. The speed of the Moon's Nodes lies between that of Jupiter (with a period of 12 years) and Saturn (with a period of ca. 29 years). What this means in practice is that different people have different positions of the Moon's Nodes, which adds considerably to the interest of the subject.

The line of nodes is the line drawn between the Ascending and the Descending Nodes, which are always in exact opposition. The Nodes have been recognized as a significant element from ancient times, because of their connection with eclipses of the Sun and Moon. When the Moon and Sun approach the line of nodes (not further away than 9° or 12° as the case may be), there is an eclipse.

Ever since their discovery more than 4000 years ago, the Nodes have been treated as real entities with a regular and uniform motion of their own, even though it has long been realized that they are not actual bodies in space. For the Nodes are not material objects, but points of intersection lying in two orbital planes. Telescopes cannot be focused on them to measure them. They were inferred from eclipses; and then, after prolonged observation of the eclipse cycle, it became possible to calculate an average value of their motion. Astrologers still use the mean motion of the "current Moon's Ascending Node" (ca. 3 minutes of arc per day).

However, for some time, we have been capable of calculating the true motion of the Moon's Nodes (by allowing for perturbations in the Moon-Earth-Sun system). And it turns out that they swing backward and forward in a very pronounced manner, and, indeed, may be retrograde for several days. The difference between the true Node and the average Node can be as much as 2-1/2 degrees.

Clearly, such a large difference ought not to be ignored in astrological practice. Therefore we have carried out a careful investigation in order to discover which of these values for the Node is more relevant psychologically. Our results have left us in no doubt that the true value yields much more precise and reliable information than the mean value does. This can easily be verified in horoscopes where there are aspects to one of the positions given for the Node but not to the other.

The names Dragon's Head and Dragon's Tail for the Ascending and Descending Nodes, respectively, stem from the mythological thinking of the past. Ancient people were unnerved when an eclipse of the Sun or Moon intruded on the cosmic order. They imagined that the Sun or Moon had been seized by a dreadful dragon and swallowed into its dark interior. The dragon voided them after a while, but anyone who witnessed an eclipse of the Sun or Moon underwent a profound spiritual experience. Here, too, we have the beginnings of astrology.

Stonehenge—the First Lunar Calendar

At the threshold of astrology—as we can say with certainty today—stands religious admiration and painstaking observation of the Moon and of its remarkable movements and phases. This is proved by the earliest signs of human culture in various parts of the world; namely in paleolithic cave paintings and in megalithic burial chambers, monoliths, menhirs, and stone circles.

One of the most important of these early cultural monuments is the so-called "megalithic astrocomputer" of Stonehenge, on Salisbury plain in the South of England. It consists of several rings of gigantic stones, and of artificial ramparts and mounds; all laid out in accordance with the results of centuries of observations of the motions of the Sun and Moon, and in such a way that all the conspicuous phenomena of the two Lights could be predicted. The alignments of the artificial landmarks were oriented to the Sun

and Moon. And, amazingly enough, the structure can still be used
as an astronomical instrument today!

Stonehenge in its present form was built in three stages
between 2000 and 1500 B.C. (there is no way of knowing what, if anything, preceded it). Three different ethnic groups, one after the
other, lived on Salisbury plain and did the construction work. The
oldest part (Stonehenge I, ca. 2000 B.C., see plan) consists of the
outer banks with two mounds, the "Avenue" with several megaliths,
and the "Aubrey Holes." (See figure 3 below.) This part already
enabled the equinoxes (times when day and night are equal) and
the solstices (the longest and shortest days) to be determined, and
was therefore a calendar. But, what is more amazing, it predicted
every eclipse of the Sun and Moon, to the exact day and hour!

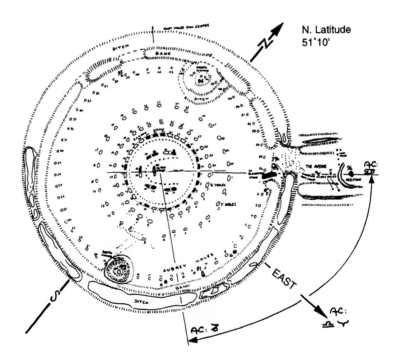

Figure 3. Stonehenge.

Although its builders must have been ignorant of the path of the Moon's Nodes, observations of the varying positions of sunrise and moonrise made by many generations would have revealed that an eclipse can occur only when the Moon rises in the path of the Sun (the ecliptic). It would also have become clear that eclipses occur at very irregular intervals and that they have a cycle of 18.61 years. This was in spite of the fact that, in those days, neither fractions nor decimals had been invented. The ring of "Aubrey Holes" (named for their discoverer, John Aubrey) served as a kind of computer (it would be quite apt to describe them as an "astronomical abacus"). The ring contains 56 holes. If, to begin with, a marker stone is placed at hole 56, and if, every year, this stone is moved by three Aubrey Holes in an anticlockwise direction, we shall find that it reaches hole 54 in eighteen years and that, the following year, a new cycle commences at hole 1. After a further eighteen years, the stone is at hole 55 and, the following year, the third cycle begins at hole 2. Finally, after another eighteen years, the stone is at hole 56 again, and so a cycle comes to a close.

By this ingenious device, the builders overcame the problem of fractions: three times 18.61 years equals 55.83 years (instead of 56). The small error produced an inaccuracy which, after 360 years, had to be corrected by moving the stone by one hole. Now, the annual displacement of the stone by three holes makes an angle of 19° 17' 08"—and this is very nearly the natural retrograde motion of the Moon's Node in one year (which is 19° 20' 08" to be exact).

And so (without observing it physically) it was possible, every year, to take a sighting of the position of the Moon's Node on the horizon. This was done along a line joining the center of the structure with the marking stone in the appropriate Aubrey hole. And, as the Moon's Node is the point of intersection of the Moon's orbit with the ecliptic, it is the only place where eclipses can occur.

By carrying out further numbering procedures in this wonderful ring of 56 stones, it would have been possible to determine the day and hour of the event; an intellectual feat that, a few years ago, would not have been credited to the so-called "primitive people" of the New Stone Age in Britain.

That Stonehenge was not only a soli-lunar calendar but, most probably, also a religious center, is evidenced by the results of various excavations, especially in the Aubrey Holes; in some of which, ashes and fragments of bone have been found—a clear indication of funeral rites. Now and then perhaps, the mortal remains of votaries of the Stonehenge cult were placed in whatever Aubrey Hole marked the Ascending Node at the moment of death—to smooth the passage of the soul to the other world.

The Moon's Node goes through a cycle; and people 4000 years ago realized this. They were profoundly affected by it. Now we take it for granted, but for them it was a gripping experience. One can imagine them trembling in awe at something they could not see but knew was there. The difficulty for us is to enter into their feelings; and so, for a long time, the Moon's Node has been very much underrated.

The Moon-Node Axis as a Line of Development

Since the Moon's Nodes—ascending and descending—are always in opposition, a Moon-Node axis exists which is significant for development. The Nodes designate a path. (See figure 4.) The Ascending Node of my chart can be thought of as lying at my feet, straight in front of me, and as representing the future. Behind me, the path runs to the Descending Node, my past into which I can retreat.

The implication of the Moon-Node line is that whatever assists "my progress" is good for me, and whatever hinders or opposes it is bad for me. The welfare of society does not enter into the question, but only what is helpful or otherwise to me. The value-system of a horoscope is completely subjective; it is not one in which everybody is treated alike. In other words its evaluation

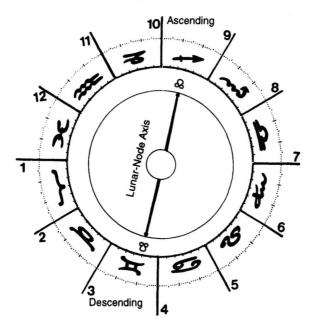

Figure 4. The Moon's Node axis.

has to do with someone called me; and only "I" know (deep down anyway) what is right or wrong for me.

The nodal axis has to do with the psychology of individual cosmic development, and the Nodes themselves are a measure of how the individual may be expected to develop. I can start splitting hairs over my thoughts, my life, and my actions, and can find excuses for much of my behavior by calling good and evil relative; but the Moon's Nodes clearly say—and something deep inside me says so, too—"Stop! No progress is possible if you continue like that." It is a warning finger laid on what is right or wrong at any given moment. This is what makes the nodal axis with the Ascending and Descending Nodes so important.

Lode-stars of the Psyche

The nodal line also divides the Moon's orbit into an upper and a lower half, beginning with the Ascending or the Descending Node as the case may be. According to Dane Rudhyar, the Ascending Node is the place of least resistance to progress in the direction of spiritual growth or maturity; the reason being that the upper sector of the lunar orbit is comparable with the visible part of the zodiac. In this sector above the horizon, the Moon is conscious in us, so to speak. We can function with it with greater awareness than when it is in the lower sector. (The reader must be careful not to jump to the wrong conclusion here. No reference is being made to the lunar phases: the above definition has nothing to do with the increase and decrease in light as the Moon waxes and wanes.)

In classical astrology, the planet or planets on the Ascendant (just above the horizon at the moment of birth) are especially significant for the native, particularly in regard to the future: they control the native's fate. In modern terms, we say that planets above the Ascendant, in the 12th house, are the individual's lode-stars, because the 12th house is the house of inner dimensions. We know scarcely anything of these in our early years, but slowly come to realize them and, in doing so, change, develop, and become more conscious.

Much the same applies to the Ascending Node. Planets in its neighborhood have special importance. They, too, may be called lode-stars of the psyche. So, in looking at our psyche and our emotional "I," we ought to pay attention to these planets. The psyche, which in the child rules the whole being, the psychic "I" which experiences and affirms itself by making contacts, this is represented by the Moon.

In contrast to the Sun, which comes to the fore as our conscious "I" and shines, grows, and expands, the Moon is our more retiring psychic "I," which has to be reflected in others for affirmation and self-consciousness. Even in adult life, the Moon is still something of a problem. Indeed, our inclination is to suppress this emotional "I" and to replace it by the Sun-ego, because we think more highly of the latter.

However, the Moon is full of activity, and the more scope it is given, the more holistic our lives will be. On the other hand, the more we repress the lunar "I," the more emotionally immature we shall become. Repression of the lunar principle when the solar "I" really starts to flourish (which should happen at 20–36 years of age) causes the emotional "I" to remain infantile, or at least to preserve some infantile traits. But, for a person to be truly adult, the lunar "I" must develop alongside the solar "I."

This holistic growth happens via the Moon's Nodes. Thus we must be sensitively perceptive in our contacts and must experience them with increasing awareness, whether they are contacts with things, situations, individuals, or living creatures of any kind. If we react to these with sensitivity, and experience our contacts with increasing differentiation, our contactual "I" will grow. The Nodes form an important dimension in this definition.

The lesson we learn from the Ascending Node is to be relaxed in our contacts, to respond to them with natural sensitivity, and to mature as we experience them. The Moon's Node helps the ego grow through the affirmation it receives; and with this growth there comes a new understanding. After each contact, we know more then we did before, not only through intellectual cognizance of the event or of its *raison d'être*, but also through direct, physical, sensory experience and perception.

The Ascending Node

The Ascending Node is the one we record in the chart, because this is the Node that represents our prospects for personal development. Its counterpart, the Descending Node is easily located, being in exact opposition to the Ascending Node (see earlier illustration). Usually, the Descending
Node need not be considered unless there is a planet either in

conjunction with it or square to it. Aspects to the Ascending Node are listed in the ephemeris, but not those to the Descending Node.

The Ascending Node is rather like a compass needle in its ability to help us find the right way to improve our character. However, it is not an all-purpose compass needle, but is special to the individual. It has to do with my personal pathway. I can become lost in the thicket of life, and be unable to see where I am going; but, on consulting the Moon's Node, I can find my bearings once more. Admittedly, this is not very easy to do, but if I look at the house position of the Moon's Node, I shall know what immediate steps I should take.

The Moon's Node is often defined as a point of contact. Usually, it is tacitly assumed that the contact will be with some individual or other. However, this is not a hard and fast rule. In many charts, the Node can certainly indicate contacts with individuals, but in others the contacts are with objects, in others again they are with situations or opportunities, and in still others they are with specific activities or occupations. In any event, what matters is that the Node is normally a point of permanent opportunity for further development. Most of the information to be derived from it lies in the nature of the house it occupies. The meaning of this house is the main meaning of the Node.

Next in importance are the aspects. The planets in aspect to it are helpful tools which can be used to initiate the course of the action indicated by the Node. Much less personal is the sign occupied by the Node, because it stays there for some 1-1/2 years. No exact explanation can be given of how the Moon's Node works, but it is really very effective as a modifying influence on the character and as a spur to personal development.

The Node is an unconscious power; but, as the individual matures, it ought eventually to discharge itself in a conscious spiritual function. It is a factor in the expansion of consciousness, generally through the experiences involved in contacts—provided the native reacts to them with sensitivity, and is determined to make the most of them.

The Descending Node

Because the Moon's Node has to do with the Moon, it touches our past, and the concrete realities in our past. Thus the Moon-Node system, and especially the Descending Node, brings to light old habits, and these can produce definite manifestations. Medieval astrology called the Ascending Node "the point of Jupiter" and the Descending Node "the point of Saturn." And there is truth in this. Jupiter is the planet of growth and expansion. Saturn, on the other hand, is associated with stagnation, with the legacy of the past, and with what has come of the native's abilities and routines. Whether the spotlight is turned on a person's youth or on former lives, these all belong to the past, treasured though they may be. Possibly they have strengths or virtues; but we have to bear in mind that, at each new stage in our development, our former talents can turn into handicaps; or, as the wise old saying puts it, "a virtue can become a vice."

After any ability has been perfected, it tends to lose its cutting edge. I can feel so happy with my skill that I no longer look round for new possibilities. And then it is that the virtue becomes a vice. This is what is really implied in the name "point of Saturn": it is a point where I can block my own development because I have lost the desire to change. And so, the Descending Node is a critical point: obvious enough, but needing to be handled with great care.

If, for example, a Node, regardless of its position in sign and house, receives nothing but red aspects, the first thing to observe is that it will be hard for the native to make use of the Ascending Node. Consequently, he or she will be inclined to take the easy way out and use the Descending Node; all the more so if there is a planet conjunct the Descending Node and in opposition to the Ascending Node (which is something we shall consider in more detail later). A similar case arises if there is a planet square the Ascending Node and square another planet that is conjunct the Descending Node. Then we have a "T-Square," and this always denotes a closed mind. The individual feels more or less compelled to follow the beaten track.

The Rhythm of the Moon's Nodes

As we have already said, the Ascending Node is the only one we mark in the horoscope, because it is the point that represents the possibility of further development; whereas the Descending Node represents the past and its affairs, and indicates what we have already learned and can do with ease. The Descending Node, therefore, is a point where no further development is possible, a point of stoppage. If it is true that "to stand still is to retreat," then it is also a place of retreat. Nevertheless, the nodal axis, the connecting line between the nodes, which are always in opposition, indicates a rhythmic process.

The Moon is full of rhythm: the rhythm of waxing and waning, of ebb and flow, of the rise and fall of the Earth's surface, of birth and death. Therefore, in approaching the Ascending Node, our way ahead in life, we should combine it with the Descending Node in a rhythm suitable to us. For the most part, this rhythm will be regulated by the deliberate cultivation of openness to the Ascending Node; but, just as on a journey there is a natural pattern of travel and rest, so we can unwind periodically with the Descending Node as we would with friends.

Thus we must clearly distinguish between a more unconscious, reflex response to life and a more conscious, personally controlled life. Of course, there are dangers inherent in the Descending, or reflex-working, Node, but we must bear in mind that, properly handled, the Descending Node becomes a point of rest, a resource on which we can always fall back, a place of renewal, an opportunity to regress which is not merely sometimes allowed but is even necessary. But the right proportion has to be discovered, the rhythm that is best for us; which is where the "art of living" comes in.

The Moon's Node and the Ascendant

The Ascendant is one of the factors that has to be considered when we are looking at the Moon's Node in the horoscope. It gives us a better understanding of the Moon-Node compass needle, which always points us in a certain direction. By furnishing a wider framework, it enables us to understand why the Node is as it is and not otherwise. The Ascendant and the Nodes go together thematically. The Nodes mark the intersection of two planes, and the Ascendant and Descendant also mark the intersection of two planes: our horizon and the ecliptic (the Zodiac). The east-point on our horizon, where the signs rise, is called the Ascendant; the west-point is where they set, and is called the Descendant.

There is a fine saying by Lao Tzu: "A journey of a thousand miles began with a single step."[1] I can contemplate such a journey, but I will not make it as long as I do not take the first step. Our life proceeds from many first steps.

In the Ascendant and the Moon's Node we have two reminders of Lao Tzu's saying. The Ascendant is a destination-board spelling out the goal of my inner life. Many are unaware of their goal, yet they struggle toward it. During their lives, they automatically follow the route that has been laid down for them, like tourists in a national park. They move along a path without thinking. The Ascendant is both the goal and the way. It shows the quality that has to be developed if the goal is to be reached. As our distant objective, it beckons us. During our lives, we tend to develop the qualities of our rising signs. Nevertheless, it is sometimes hard for us to know how to proceed when there seem to be no clues. Now the Ascending Node supplies the clues for taking the first step; it points out the right direction. The Moon's Node is consistent. It shows what to do, and what measures to adopt in the face of difficulties. It reveals the things and attitudes that promote

---

[1] *The Sayings of Lao Tzu,* translated by Lionel Giles (London: John Murray, 1937), p. 37.

growth. It is a sign post that is always there, even when the terminus is out of sight.

There are some very practical things I can do if I want to get the best out of my Node: I can adopt a realistic approach, open to what is new. I can ask myself, "With this Ascendant, what is expected of me? What is the object of my development?" In some situations, it may require too much effort to look as far ahead as the Ascendant; but, at least, I can see what the Moon's Node is indicating. Admittedly, in theoretical astronomy, the Ascendant is well defined. Astronomically, the horizon is a near point. Nevertheless, when I approach it, it invariably recedes and moves elsewhere. From the point of view of the universe, my horizon is very near me, but as a goal it is unattainable. Just as I suppose I am about to reach it, I find that it is as far away as ever. Therefore it continually calls for further growth and movement.

On the other hand, the Node is outside the Earth and astronomically much further off. The horizon is ca. 4–5 miles away, but the Node is situated in the Moon's orbit, 240,000 miles away from the Earth.

Thus the values are reversed. The Moon's Node, far out in space, shows something quite obvious, something I can do here and now; the Ascendant shows the distant goal. In the horoscope, this means that a native who, for example, has the Node on the left part of the chart, in the "I" region, would do better not to travel round the globe looking for a starting point; but, drawing on his or her personal reserves should practice introspection. But if the Node is on the right of the horoscope, in the "You" region, then the native should—indeed must—go out into the world of humanity to find the proper place from which to advance.

Exercise on the Moon's Node— its Relationship to the Ascendant

The following exercise on the relationship between the Node and the Ascendant is worth performing: try to see the qualitative relationship between these two elements in various horoscopes. How does the first step tie in with "the goal a thousand miles away"? What do the two points have in common? Often they occupy very different regions of the chart. Often the definitions of the two points appear to be at variance, e.g., when the Node is in a sign or house that not only does not harmonize with the sign on the Ascendant, but has a completely different nature (e.g., when the Ascendant is in a Fire sign and the Moon's Node is in a Water sign). Discrepancies such as these will prove to be troublesome initially, but it is striking how the two points cohere, even so; how, in fact, the first step, which the Moon's Node challenges the native to take, leads to the goal suggested by the Ascendant. The following example will make this clearer. See Chart 1 on page 20.

The Ascending Node is in the 12th house. Obviously, in this horoscope, it counterbalances the stellium in the 8th house, and is thus a corrective element in the character. With Leo heavily tenanted in the 8th house, the native craves public recognition to give him a sense of worth; but the Moon's Node suggests that he should make a deliberate effort to be more retiring. Since, for him, the first step involves the 12th house, he must learn to bear solitude. Whenever problems or conflicts arise, he should go somewhere quiet to consider the next step introspectively. In other words, he should voluntarily let go of external fixations and involvement with others. The native needs to retire to a quiet place from time to time, to work out what he expects of others, what they want from him, and what are his real needs.

This interior reflection provides a safe retreat, where he is free and independent, and can try to scale the highest spiritual peaks—as befits his Capricorn Ascendant. He must learn to be on his own, and to abandon his dependence on others. This will lead to the individuation process of Capricorn, and to initiation into

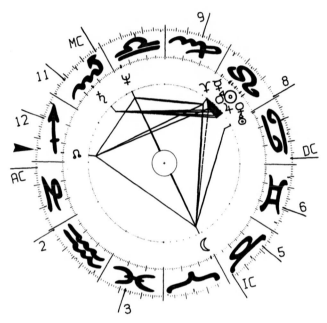

Chart 1. Example horoscope, August 9, 1955, 17:16, Zürich, Switzerland. Koch houses.

the secrets of life during a lonely mountain-top experience. Afterward there must come an inner reversal, a descent from the mountain so that others can be shown the way up. Having traveled so far, the native may well become a true leader. After the inner change and the ascent, he ought always be prepared to go to the crowd in order to show others how to reach the top. Indeed, time and again, he will clearly see their basic needs and what it is he can give them.

All this is in tune with the esoteric keynote of Capricorn: "I am engrossed in celestial light, yet turn my back on this light."

Having interpreted our Node, we can use it for guidance, and shall no doubt see an obvious connection between the Node and the quality of the Ascendant. The existence of a relationship between the Moon's Node and the Ascendant can be verified in living experience, provided we bear in mind that the Ascendant is more abstract and remote than the Node.

When it is given prominence, the Ascendant becomes the mask we learn to wear to face the world. It is a role we play. If we are wise, we will avoid identifying with it; for to do so is to remain ignorant of our true selves. From a spiritual standpoint, it is the distant goal, the quality by which the soul will become active at the end of life. As an aid to understanding this spiritual quality of the Rising Sign, an esoteric keynote such as the one quoted above can be employed for each sign of the zodiac.

The Moon's Node as an Ameliorating Element

A very important point is the ameliorating, compensating element in the Moon's Node. Each horoscope has a basic tendency, which is to be inferred from the chart as a whole, not from a single stellium.

A horoscope that has its center of gravity on the right suggests that the native is outward-looking, and actively or passively involved in the world around. The environment, and everything to do with it, and the give and take that goes on between people, profoundly interests this person, who is more or less dependent on the environment. This leads to overcompensation of the ego, and increasing reliance on others. There can even be an identity-loss if personal identity becomes so dependent on encouragement, confirmation, or applause from those around, that it loses its autonomy.

---

[2]For further details, see the book by Louise Huber, *Reflections & Meditations on the Signs of the Zodiac* (Tempe, AZ: American Federation of Astrologers, 1984).

In a case such as this, the Moon's Node can (for example) occupy the 1st house and correct the faulty behavior. The Node in the 1st house urges: "You must be yourself, you must have the courage to stand up for yourself and say, 'Look at me, please, and accept me as I am.'" Now this is very important where the aspect picture emphasizes the right side of the chart. The Node would have an ameliorating tendency because it would tend to counterbalance the main weight of the character and prevent its extreme development. In short, it would help to keep the identity intact.

That is one example of how the Node can have a compensating effect where there is one-sidedness in the natal chart. The one-sidedness can be due to some planet or group of planets, or to a general tendency—as in the above-mentioned emphasis of the right side. It is important always to bear in mind that the Node has this regulatory function and is therefore a factor in the horoscope that stands for psychological health.

Chapter 2

Aspects to the Moon's Node

What are aspects? • Red Aspects • Conjunction • Square •
Opposition • Blue Aspects • Green Aspects • The Node and
the Planets • The Node with the Moon • The Node with the
Sun • The Node with Saturn • The Node with Mercury • The
Node with Venus • The Node with Mars • The Node with
Jupiter • The Node with Uranus • The Node with Neptune • The
Node with Pluto • Unaspected Moon's Nodes • The Moon's
Node as Leading Planet • The Node in the Three House
Sectors • Intercepted Signs •

What are Aspects?

Aspects are lines of force and connecting paths; they are avenues of approach from one planet to another. The planets naturally interact through the aspects. The Moon's Node is in a somewhat different category: it makes no aspects, since it is not itself a planetary body but a reference point. However, it can be aspected. In other words, aspects can travel from planets to the Node but never in the reverse direction. Thus the Node has no orb (range on either side of it over which a given aspect could influence it). Aspects to the Moon's Node are by way of being lines of sight from the planets; or, to put it another way, they are a sort of commentary on the Node made by some planet. For example: "What the Node wants is wonderful?" or, "I'll have nothing to do with that idea!" Aspects can signify liking, endorsement, and support, or ambivalence, uncertainty, and even aversion, in regard to what is signified by the Node.

The aspects do not each have a single, universally applicable, definition, because allowance must always be made for the conscious choice of the native where the Moon's Node is concerned. An individual who from higher motives consciously works on self, will not respond to (and turn to account) aspects of the Node in the same way as the individual who, rather instinctively, lives for self. The descriptions given here—and this should be borne in mind in everything that follows—are of the unconscious, reflex, type of response to aspects of the Moon's Node.

We classify aspects in three groups to which we give the color labels, red, blue and green. The red aspects are conjunctions, oppositions, and squares. A proviso has to be made in the case of conjunctions, which do have their soft side and are not typical red aspects. The blue aspects are trines and sextiles. The green aspects are quincunxes and semisextiles.

Red Aspects

Conjunction	0°
Opposition	180°
Square	90°

Conjunction (0 degrees)

Planets conjunct the Moon's Node must be taken very seriously as far as personal development is concerned. They can be applied immediately to our spiritual progress. Also these planets indicate how we behave in contacts. If they are sensitive planets (Mercury, Jupiter, the Moon, and Neptune), we allow ourselves to be influenced by others; if they are hard planets (the Sun, Mars, Saturn, Uranus and Pluto), we impose ourselves on others, telling them what to do and how to behave. The planets that occupy the same place as the Node can cause problems, however. For example, if the planets associated with the Node are sensitive, like the Moon or Neptune, we may also be sensitive, or even hypersensitive. I shall have more to say later about individual planets in conjunction with, and in opposition to, the Moon's Node.

When a career is being chosen, it is important to note any planets conjunct the Node in the birth chart. Usually they point to special abilities according to their nature. For example, the Node directly motivates sensitive planets in this aspect by stimulating a deep desire to serve.

Opposition (180 degrees)

Red aspects, especially oppositions, have an antipathy to the Moon's Ascending Node: "What it wants won't do at all for me, it is too much of a strain," says the planet making this aspect. A planet in opposition to the Ascending Node is also conjunct the Descending Node.

In a red aspect, there is a tendency to bring the Descending Node into play by reflex action, because it is irksome to use the Ascending Node. Red aspects do not favor the Ascending Node, but reinforce the Descending Node. In an opposition to the Ascending Node, I am liable to resist the planet that forms the opposition. What is more, I am inclined to ignore, deny, or repress the opportunity to make progress. The opposition is often a repression aspect. I simply lock something up in my unconscious. Two elements are confronting one another and tend to be mutually exclusive. Either there is a block with neither side budging, or else the partner in the opposition is chosen and the other side is repressed. It is obstructed, projected on the outside world, seen as hostile, and repelled by defense mechanisms. The reverse of repression is hyperactivity—this is more usual with squares, but may occur with oppositions when they are from active planets.

The Square (90 degrees)

Squares, too, frequently give rise to rejection and defense. A square to the Ascending Node always partners a square to the Descending Node, and these combine to form a T-square. The chief tendency here is to take flight in the direction opposite to the Ascending Node's developmental goal. The native who has such a square readily engages in hectic activity that is often meaningless, and in activity for its own sake. He or she simply has to keep busy, but has little sense of purpose; finding it easy to run round in circles and get nowhere—every now and then having to stop and wait for the next opportunity. Now there is nothing gained by taking the short cut offered by the Descending Node. A great deal of insight and strength are required, if one is to profit by the square. When a square falls on the Moon's Node from a planet, further development is avoided. The potential in the Ascending Node or in the planet, is avoided, opposed, and criticized; it is treated ambivalently. This is because of the inevitable second square, which is to the Descending Node—the partner in the T-square.

When, for example, there is a T-square from the Ascending Node to a Sun-Moon opposition, a red grand cross exists which includes the Descending Node. The resultant figure is full of tension and is "karmic." If, in addition, the Ascending Node is in a fixed sign, it will not make a good launching pad. A figure of this type usually has a restraining influence, and the native stays put just to be on the safe side. To make progress would inevitably entail leaving behind old structures or established certainties. If the person with a square to the Moon's Node runs true to form, he or she will wrestle with the problem instead of being relaxed, and will engage in hectic activity—more often than not quite unprofitably.

Now the contacts represented by the Moon require sensitivity and understanding toward the contact partner or object. They require a relaxed attitude that is either outgoing or receptive, according to whether the individual is extravert or introvert. The idea is not to make a contact, but to let it happen and to experience it. The person who makes and manipulates contacts, repels people. If the Moon's Node is as described above, the native will tend to acknowledge contacts mechanically instead of experiencing them subjectively as deeply as possible. In the case of the opposition, he or she will simply hold back; but, where there is a T-square, the native will hover between inhibition and hyperactivity.

Blue Aspects

Sextile   60°
Trine   120°

Blue aspects confirm the theme of the Moon's Node. The "first step" depends very much on the disposition of the native, who often is too idle to make a move without outside stimulus.

Trines show keen faculties and bring about a completely natural organic development, because the person seizes his or her chances, often unconsciously, at a moderate rate of progress. There is a "nose," so to speak, for useful opportunities.

Usually, in sextiles, the way forward is not turned into something hard or strenuous, but takes a natural course. Often the native makes the most of leisure moments and misses certain opportunities for further development. Then, later on, he or she has to go looking for them.

In blue-red aspects the Node is ambivalent. There are conflicting possibilities, and this can prove irritating. Sometimes the blue aspect may be chosen, sometimes the red, or the individual may do nothing at all. He or she can keep on going here and there, and can do all sorts of things, without ever doing what is needful. Patience is required to "thread a needle."

Green Aspects

Semisextile   30°
Quincunx   150°

The green aspects have to do with becoming conscious. In the minor green aspect (semisextile)
there is often a measure of uncertainty until sufficient information has been gathered. The long
green aspect (quincunx) indicates conscious problem-solving.
Every effort has to be made to find solutions. Thus what is indicated is a decision-making process through which the individual
must find himself or herself.

Severe tensions can also occur in green aspects, especially
when there is a red aspect, too. Usually there is a wavering
between polarities until a decision can be taken. A brave effort is
made to act consistently, but without success. Opportunities are
frequently missed and have to be waited for in the hope that they
will recur. Awareness and self-criticism are particularly needful
here, and questions should be asked such as: "What is happen-
ing?" or: "Why am I making no progress, have I gone wrong somewhere?" Green aspects are searching and probing aspects.

The Node and the Planets

Most Nodes receive more than one aspect and, when they do, it is
relevant to inquire which planets give which possibilities. (See
Table 1 on page 29.) The planet or planets aspecting the Moon's
Node are the instruments available to us for taking the first step
already described. Our reactions will be in keeping with the planet or planets concerned, and will vary accordingly, but the goal
toward which we move must lie where the Node is. And that is
determined by the sign and (so experience teaches) the house.
There are three things to consider in any aspect:

Table 1. The Planets.

		CREATIVE INTELLIGENCE	UNIVERSAL LOVE	SPIRITUAL WILL
DEVELOPMENTAL SPHERE — ASPIRATIONS — SPIRITUAL GROWTH	Spiritual plane — The superconscious	MOTHER ⊙ IMAGO — Occultist, Methodology, Ideal of the perfect world, SYSTEMATIZATION	CHILD ♆ IMAGO — Mystic, Mediality, Ideal of unconditional love, SERVICE	FATHER ♇ IMAGO — Magus, Metamorphosis, Ideal of human perfection, CREATION
PERSONALITY (EGO)	Personal plane — The conscious	BODY — SELF-RELIANCE ♄	EMOTIONS — YOU-CONSCIOUSNESS ☽	INTELLECT — SELF-CONSCIOUSNESS ⊙
ROLES OF THE "I" — INTERESTS AND MOTIVATIONS		Immunity — Security, Economy — Shutting, MOTHER — Heteronomous	Sensitivity — Sympathy, Learning — Opening, CHILD — Ambivalent	Vitality — Mind power, Growth — Radiating, FATHER — Autonomous
DRIVES + INSTINCT = ACHIEVEMENTS	Physical plane — The unconscious	ENJOYMENT — AESTHETIC ♀	LEARNING — COMBINATORY SENSORY ☿ ♃	WORK — MOTOR ♂
LIFE-PRESERVING FUNCTIONS		Assimilation, Selection, Woman, Fruitfulness	Formulation, Evaluation, Information, Perception, Human being, Impressionability	Performance, Activity, Man, Potency
ANALOGIES		Feminine, Matter, The Spirit, Siva	Neuter, Consciousness, The Son, Vishnu	Masculine, Mind, The Father, Brahma

1. Planetary qualities that are linked with the Node ought to be encouraged and employed in everyday life. But they should never be used for self-glorification.

2. These planetary qualities are often helpful to the career. The planet that is conjunct the Node can indicate the profession that would suit us best. Each profession is a pathway of self-development; and, as the Node has to do with our development, the planet concerned will obviously have a bearing on the profession.

3. We should make a point of deliberately working with the planets that make aspects to the Nodes. It is important to practice self-observation and to discover one's bad habits and indulgences. The places of least resistance for spiritual ascent always require the maximum human effort.

As already mentioned, conjunctions or oppositions to the Moon's Node are particularly important for spiritual development. These aspects will be described later.

The Node with the Moon

When there is a conjunction with the Moon, the sensitivity is greater, contacts are taken very seriously, and the native is occupied by emotional matters. Therefore the development of the capacity for friendship and love comes very much to the fore. Love and affection, pampering and dependence are experienced intensely. Because the Moon is a fluctuating emotional element, reversals are often suffered, and there is hurt and disappointment when a cooling off of love and affection occurs followed by disregard.

In an opposition of the Moon to the Node, we have a possibility of insincere contacts, according to whether or not the Moon is on the right or left side of the horoscope. If it is on the right, there will be numerous contacts, but they may be inappropriate; that is to say, they may impede instead of assisting the native. Many cannot live without contacts and are constantly hopping from one relationship to another. If the Moon is on the left, or I-side, the contacts will certainly be fewer. Then it is important to try to come out of one's shell, because the Ascending Node is on the right and its ascent takes place via the "You." In each opposition, one should make use of the sphere of life represented by the house occupied by the Ascending Node.

This will cost effort, because the Descending Node which, of course, is conjunct the Moon, responds by encouraging a strongly reflex, almost mechanical form of behavior. The native is repeatedly entangled in contacts of the same type as before, yet never realizes it.

The Node with the Sun

The conjunction with the Sun places the self-consciousness of the native in the foreground. What matters here is to function autonomously and independently, to develop the character traits and strengths that already exist, and to concentrate on the achievement of personal goals. With the Sun's aspects, personal commitment to all affairs of the house or axis is required. The emphasis is always laid on individual effort for further development; imperfections or weaknesses are not tolerated. Given freedom and independence, the native will attain his or her objective and will make solid progress.

In the opposition, negative ego-forces often come into play. The natives are full of self-admiration and believe they have full control of everything represented by the axis concerned. Many of them are conceited and proud, and lay claim to being unique when (in most instances) they are not. They refuse to admit that they possess the weaknesses of the sign involved, and believe that, being already sufficiently developed, they have no need to work on themselves. Often, these people feel that they are being neglected and imagine that they are tremendously important, although, usually this is mere self-deception. They have a tendency towards monomania.

The Node with Saturn

In aspects of Saturn to the Moon's Node, there is a significant difference between the conjunction and the opposition. In the conjunction, each step in the native's development is carefully weighed, and everything is treated very seriously. Nothing is done on impulse, and many natives wait a long time before they move forward: they doubt and hesitate, and are unable to act with spontaneity. Even after making a great effort, they believe that they have done nothing and are simply not good enough. Because the basic principle of Saturn is security, they live in dread of doing something wrong, and often delay unnecessarily before taking the next step.

In the opposition, Saturn stands at its own point: for, in the classical literature of astrology, the Descending Node is also "the point of Saturn." Here it hinders the native's progress considerably, and the latter clings to old habits and fails to see the need for change. The native is liable to regress, and refuses to strike out in a new direction. Many are pessimistic and do not believe that there is a better life for them. They load themselves with needless responsibilities and are hardly free to act. Many take refuge in duty, and imagine they have to do everything and that, without them "nothing would ever get done." With Saturn on the nodal axis it is hard to break old habits: there is a constant temptation to lapse into familiar reactions and routines.

The Node with Mercury

In the conjunction, the learning function is activated, and development is rapid. According to the placement in sign and house, the native is eager to learn, versatile, and curious, and glad to pursue further development. The powers of expression are above average, friendships are readily formed—and just as readily broken if they impede personal advancement.

In the opposition, Mercury can produce loquacity. The native humors others, has no fixed opinion, and is easily influenced. Depending on the house or sign, he or she can resort to lies born of sensation-seeking and willingness to compromise, and can be landed in unpleasant situations. Arguments employed are far-fetched, and refuge is taken in sophistry.

The Node with Venus

The conjunction encourages the native to make many friends and to be very obliging. With Venus, a person will want to enjoy the good things of life and will avoid hard work if at all possible. Artistic gifts are often present. However, Venus can be a hindrance to the Ascending Point, because this demands conscious effort on the individual's part. Although the planet promotes the feminine aspect of love, upward progress is often impeded.

In the opposition, slowing down is even more marked. There are a dislike of exertion, reliance on others, and the view that making a token effort is good enough. According to the theme of the axis, the native waits to be motivated by others, and is dependent on stronger, usually male, persons. The love of ease and a tendency to compromise, mean that many opportunities for personal growth are allowed to slip by, and that refuge is taken in pseudo-harmony.

The Node with Mars

In the conjunction, Mars is experienced as a powerful driving force for progress. The personal advance upward is courageous, although unsuitable means are frequently used. The native has ambition and does not mind the trouble involved in undertaking unusual tasks; which often tax the strength, yet are carried out with energy and enthusiasm. Depending on the sign and house involved, the Martian force brushes aside all opposition, is often incensed by it, and can then put personal development first with a big show of aggression and egocentricity.

In the opposition, the militant energies can prevail. According to the sign and house, the native will tilt at windmills and mis-

direct his or her energies. Wrong ideas are fiercely defended, but
without convincing others of their merit. Many resort to feverish
activity and waste their strength. The time that must elapse before
the native learns the most profitable use of the latter depends
largely on other planets aspecting Mars.

The Node with Jupiter

In the conjunction, the sensory awareness of Jupiter lends an
increased perceptiveness to the personal ascent. The natives have
a "good nose" for favorable opportunities, find themselves in the
right place at the right time and make good use of it. They keep
meeting people who are helpful to their development. Jupiter also
imparts an optimistic outlook on life, and an inclination to see the
good in people and to believe that the formative forces of evolution are at work in all. Making upward progress is relatively easy. It
was not without reason that the Ascending Node was called the
"Point of Jupiter" in the classical literature of the subject.

In the opposition, we can find the extreme pessimist instead
of the extreme optimist: someone with absolutely no belief in the
good in people or in the progress of humanity. At the Descending
Node the forces of Saturn are especially active, and they hamper
Jupiter with its awareness of what is meaningful. Depending on
the sign, the native can always find an excuse for personal weaknesses and can believe, "That is not really me." Many are "doubt-
ing Thomases." They throw up the sponge as soon as difficulties
arise. It is hard for them to look on the bright side.

The Node with Uranus

The conjunction gives a perpetual desire to outgrow one's limitations, and to transcend the borders of the known. The aim is
expansion of consciousness in order to find greater security and a

more harmonious way of life through new knowledge. Personal development is taken very seriously, and novel methods of accelerating it are sought. The individual identifies with the spirit of the age and with borderland knowledge. Uranus often brings about development abruptly, through sudden events.

In the opposition, the natives follow a zig-zag path, and imagine that it is possible to clear obstacles at a single bound. They try to avoid the inhibiting forces of Saturn that threaten to pin them down. Nevertheless, many of them believe that they have made no progress in spite of all their efforts. At such moments they are in danger of becoming resigned to failure and of giving everything up. Then, when Uranus swings into action again and starts turning things upside down, what was once thought to be good can be rejected, and vice versa. Barriers are rushed, curtains are torn down—often on the spur of the moment.

The Node with Neptune

The conjunction gives full scope in contacts to an all-embracing love of humanity. The native is ready to give up all for love, and believes in universal philanthropy and in spiritual freedom. Many take up social work in the belief that the only way for them to develop is by caring for the sick or for the underprivileged. As a matter of fact, the Neptunian sensitivity frequently leads them to forget their own development as they work and sacrifice themselves for others. Nevertheless, the boundary-removing principle of Neptune can do much to promote spiritual development.

In the opposition, various snares can lie along the path of development. There is a naïve faith in promises of all sorts, and a tendency to fall prey to cheats and swindlers. Because the natives are only vaguely aware of their limitations, they are apt to make mistakes, become enmeshed in intrigues, and have difficulty in finding a plan of personal development. The ego-disintegration due to Neptune often results in diffuse aims.

The Node with Pluto

The conjunction with Pluto will activate the Node and initiate the first step in personal development. Everything with which it comes in contact is intensified. The natives strive for personal and spiritual growth. Many (according to the sign and house involved) put all their eggs in one basket, develop an inflated idea of their own importance, and have an inner urge to achieve something exceptional. With Pluto, there seems to be an inner calling, and a powerful motivation towards self-improvement and growth in maturity. However, power is also desired for its own sake, and further development may be sought in order to gain more influence over others. In the opposition, the will-power is employed selfishly and often roughly too. The ego-transformation which should be produced by Pluto stagnates, and then erupts with a breaking of old rules, a bringing of repressions into the open, and a sweeping aside of obstacles. With Pluto at the point of Saturn, the native can insist on old rights, and can lay arrogant and aggressive claims to authority. Vandalism and acts of violence perpetrated with a show of legality are other manifestations.

Unaspected Moon's Nodes

An unaspected, separately functioning Node behaves like an unaspected planet. In the first place, one does not know that one has a Node, since there is no access to it through aspects. There are no direct links with the instruments (planets) that could be used to control it. (See Chart 2.) And so there is no sure instinct for what needs to be done immediately; everything is very hit-and-miss. On many occasions, opportunities are not seen straight away and are therefore missed. Nevertheless, although this happens so often, there are also many occasions on which the proper course of action is taken, even though the conviction is lacking that the right thing is really being done. Equally, one can come out at the wrong end and not know why.

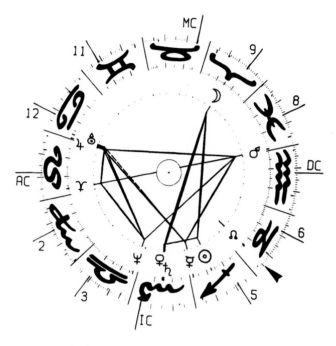

Chart 2. Example horoscope. December 5, 1954, 21:40, Wädenswil, Switzerland. Koch houses.

People with unaspected nodes may expect to be guided by their partners, who will soon make up their minds for them. Often the Node is aspected by some of the partner's planets or makes a "house or sign conjunction" with them. In the case of separately functioning planets, the native does have to deal with things, in spite of delegating so much to the partner. Primarily, the Moon's Node acts on the conscious mind; therefore the individual must care for his or her own development. Once this is understood, it is easier to come to grips with what the Node represents and to apply it with greater awareness. It helps if the Node has an aspect in the house chart. Nevertheless, one can certainly perceive a completely unaspected Node if one knows how to do so. As we have already seen, the Moon's Node is like a gap through which one can squeeze into a site that has been boarded up (the proverbial "eye of a needle"). It is an opening through which it is possible to pass unceremoniously. The Node always signifies things within reach, not far-away things like those signified by the Ascendent. The message of the Node is practical: "Do this," or, better still, "Be open to this, pay attention to it. Be prepared!"

Many people with isolated Nodes find it hard to believe in their own potential. They are always full of self-doubt. Opportunities pass them by, simply because their conscious minds fail to register them. Persons of this sort are manipulated from outside, and need repeated urging to "try again." Natives whose Node is isolated are likely to experiment with their lives and to undertake fresh ventures until, ultimately, they know enough to extract something positive out of negative experiences. Such people may say, "Yes, I'm always stuck in the same place; I work as hard as I can, but I never get anywhere." This state of mind can be very draining. Suppose, for example, that the Node is in the 9th house, the individual might question the meaning of his or her existence and start to pine away. That would be an extreme case, of course.

The effects of the unaspected Node are among the most striking proofs that the Node is an inherent element of the character: otherwise it would not be so influential. Incidentally, we must always look out for conjunctions with the Age Point, as these help to make the unaspected Node conscious.[1]

---

[1]See also Huber, *Lifeclock* (York Beach, ME: Samuel Weiser, 1994). This book was originally published in two volumes, *Lifeclock, Volume 1: Age Progression in the Horoscope* (Samuel Weiser, 1982) and *Lifeclock, Volume 2: Practical Techniques for Counseling Age Progression in the Horoscope* (Samuel Weiser, 1986). The revised edition includes an index.

The Moon's Node as Leading Planet

As is well-known, the leading planet in the horoscope sets the theme with which the native must come to terms. Whether or not the person does what the theme suggests and, if so, how, is up to him or her; except when the Node is leader. See Chart 3 on page 40. Then there is no free choice, but the theme has to be tackled. The above example, where the native's chart has the Moon's Node in the 12th house, shows this quite clearly. This individual simply must deal with the area of life represented by the house occupied by the Ascending Node, whether he or she likes it or not; avoiding it will delay development.

To misinterpret a leading planet is not a serious mistake; but to misinterpret the Node is. To this extent the Moon's Node has the last word, although it does not compel us. In the final analysis, no single element is a determining factor in the chart. However, the Node ought to be taken seriously; for it assists the native's further development. It is always meaningful and has a general balancing function. Above all, when leader, it possesses a high corrective value, because then it nearly always opposes the entire aspect picture, and its tendency is to bring about a rounding of the character and a development. Development is something specifically human. Whoever hinders his or her own development for any length of time, will slowly become ill by a psychosomatic process. Nature resists, but the Moon's Node has the last word. If a crisis occurs, the person must look to the Node to find that "gap in the fence," and to make the first step conscious. This is the way to progress, and to find a solution fairly quickly.

The Node in the Three House Sectors

By dividing each house into three dynamic sectors, we are able to determine the specific house intensities of the planets. At the cusps, the planetary forces can flow into the environment (extroversion). From the (IP) Invert Point to the (LP) Low Point, a plan-

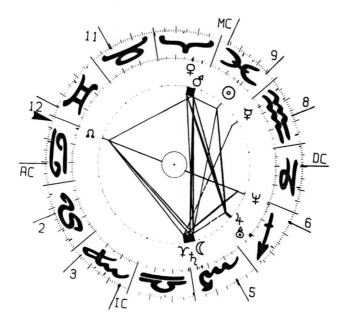

Chart 3. Example horoscope. March 3, 1983, 13:15, Kreuth, Germany. Koch houses.

et finds itself in the fixed, closed sector and tends toward consolidation (introversion). After the Low Point, there begins the arduous climb to the next house cusp; the so-called "stress sector" carries within it the possibilities of resignation or over-exertion, not to mention the associated tendencies to compensate. See figure 5.[2]

---

[2]For further information, see our book, *The Astrological Houses* (York Beach, ME: Samuel Weiser, 1978, 1984), p. 94.

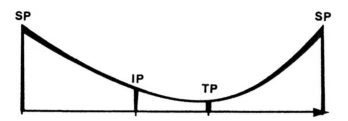

Figure 5. The three house sectors.

The House Cusp

We specify the region belonging to the axis or cusp as lying between a point just before the cusp on the one hand and the Invert Point on the other hand. The nearer the Moon's Node is to the cusp of a house, the more certain what is indicated by the Node becomes. Good use should be made of this house for the native's development; otherwise he or she will suffer repeatedly from the hard knocks of fate.

The Fixed Region

When it occupies the sector between the Invert Point and the Low Point, the Moon's Node has to do with consciousness, whatever the house may be; and introspection and self-examination are promoted because every Low Point is inward-looking.

The Low-Point Sector

The Moon's Node is fairly indifferent to Low Point positions. If a planet happens to be in opposition to the Descending Node say, the Low Point placement is found to be particularly awkward, i.e., there is a blockage. In such a constellation, the planet in opposition to the Node must be more or less forgotten and other possibilities (such as aspects to the Ascending Node from other planets) need to be considered. Although the Moon's Node is not very vigorous at the Low Point, the native does have to cultivate inner rather than outer activity.

The Stress Sector (before a house cusp)

Placement in the stress sector between the Low Point and a point just before the cusp, produces a discordant function. We are affected by the action of the house in which the Node is placed, but also by the action of the following house. There is an attraction to this next house; yet a holding back from it. The native is compelled to serve two masters. Both house themes have to be expressed: the house occupied by the Node represents obligation, and the following house represents aspiration and will. The obligations of the house actually occupied must not be neglected, although little benefit is to be hoped for from them. Nevertheless, one dare not give up, even when one has the feeling of getting nowhere in spite of one's best endeavors. This region is a stress zone for the Node. A Node right in front of the cusp of the 2nd house, for example, is in a place of stress where self is still the main concern (1st house) but, at the same time, there is a growing interest in acquiring possessions (2nd house). The native has to start integrating his or her talents—which, after all, are the most important of 2nd-house possessions—into the self-image, to give it substance and power. This task is twofold. When the Node is within one degree of the 2nd cusp, others still look at, and evaluate, the native as a person; but with increasing reference to what that person owns. Before the cusp is reached, however, the possessions are not concrete, but are internal qualities such as hidden talents. A further point is that, at this stage, success is never commensurate with effort (cf. the blue aspects).

Intercepted Signs

Planets in intercepted signs operate inwardly: it is difficult for them to externalize their energies or capabilities. They have no direct access to a house cusp to bring their energies into the world. The first step is taken internally, unseen by others. In applying these considerations to the Moon's Node, we recognize that it is not an outlet but an opening, an opening which must first be found and then used. Whether it opens inward or outward is, in principle, not of first importance; what matters is on which side of the opening one is standing.

Chapter 3

The Moon's Node
in the Houses

The First Step • The Node in the 1st House • The Node in the
2nd House • The Node in the 3rd House • The Node in the 4th
House • The Node in the 5th House • The Node in the 6th
House • The Node in the 7th House • The Node in the 8th
House • The Node in the 9th House • The Node in the 10th
House • The Node in the 11th House • The Node in the
12th House •

The First Step

The nature of the first step depends to a great extent on the nature of the house occupied by the Moon's Node. Since the Node is not a planet, we cannot expect it to do something; on the other hand it is incumbent on *us* to do something with *it*. As already mentioned, it is like a useful gap in the fence for us to find and slip through.

The main thing to do is to interpret the house placement of the Node. The attributes of the sign can then be seen as an added inner dimension. Generally speaking, the sign attributes are harder to turn to account than the house attributes are, because they exist at a deeper level, and because the signs refer to what is more qualitative and less practical. The house shows us the area of life in which we can usefully apply ourselves. It gives us an external opportunity to take the first step. Admittedly, there is also a disposition in us that does not necessarily find expression in an opportunity or situation; and this disposition is revealed by the sign. However, the directly accessible, formal starting point is always to be found in the house placement of the Moon's Node.

The twelve houses of the horoscope provide concrete information on our sphere in life and on how well we are likely to do in it; and the Node's placement by house tells us how to use this information effectively.

The Node in the 1st House

Here the individual stands out against the backdrop of his or her environment. In the 1st house the native introduces himself or herself. The 1st house is an extrovert house. The native seeks recognition and makes an effort to be noticed. With the Node in the 1st house, what is required is the courage to stand up and say, "This is what I am, and I am not going to change for anyone." See Chart 4 for an example of this placement.

When the chart is examined as a whole, it is usually found that the ego has problems in sufficiently being itself, and that this is something the Moon's Node urges us to work at. If, with the Node in the 1st house, I run into difficulties, the most likely reason is an inability to say, "Whatever happens, I am going to be myself; and it is for me to decide whether I will do a thing or not— whether or not I can do it or want to do it." With the Node in the 1st house, we must learn to stick to our point of view.

Also, it is important to be aware of the opposite Node, as there is a tendency to be ruled by the opinions of others, and to wait for them to tell us what to do. The Descending Node is, of course, in the 7th house. But reliance on someone else, and hoping that another person will pull our chestnuts out of the fire for us, so that we have no need to fight for ourselves, amounts to stagnation or falling back in development.

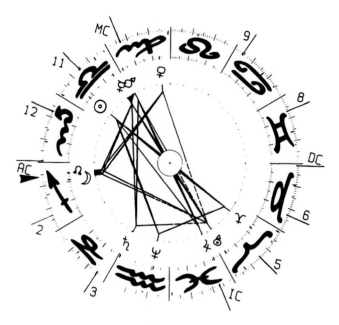

Chart 4. Friedrich Nietzsche, philosopher. *October 15, 1844, 10:00 A.M. Röcken b. Lutzen, Germany. Koch houses. Birth data from Lois M. Rodden's* The American Book of Charts *(San Diego, CA: Astro Computing Services, 1980) p. 399.*

In red aspects to the 1st-house Node, the tendency is to use the Descending Node reflexly by currying favor with the other person; we get on well with this person because we are friendly and hide the less amiable side of our character. Thus a false picture of ourself is presented, which considerably blocks our development. Certainly, in the 1st house, one has to cultivate one's image, but it should be presented as honestly as possible.

If the Node in the 1st house receives blue aspects, the partner, represented by the 7th house, will be very supportive without having to be asked. This is not as bad as when the native asks for support. The motivation is what matters. If the native tries to help himself or herself, the partner may also come along and help. That is not stagnation. Action has been taken. If the Node is on the Ascendant itself, the whole 1st-house theme must be taken very seriously. In blue aspects, and very much more so in green aspects, it is observable that often the native does not care to emphasize the ego, because it is not the "done thing." This can be a big mistake, since without parading our ego we have no real chance in the world. The world will not know who we are. It is preferable to try and make the best possible impression on people than to make none at all. The Node on the Ascendant is a place-ment in which the native almost always has to call attention to him-self or herself. The world has to be made to look at him or her. It is very important to put the self forward and to keep on improv-ing the personal image.

The Node in the 2nd House

Essentially, with the Moon's Node in the 2nd house, we are con-cerned with exploiting our capital resources. We must learn to use the possessions, capabilities, and knowledge we have acquired or partly acquired. There is no need to rely on others for their help or financial assistance. We ourselves have sufficient strength and funds to play our part in life. See Chart 5 for an example of this placement.

The 2nd house has to do with personal possessions. It is an ownership house. The individual who has the Node in the 2nd house must use what he or she owns in order to make progress. One becomes effective only when one begins to employ one's capabilities, talents, or whatever one has—material as well as intel-lectual. Generosity, too, is important to cultivate, because as a rule there is a reluctance to give; or, depending on the sign, there is not enough self-knowledge and self-confidence in what one has.

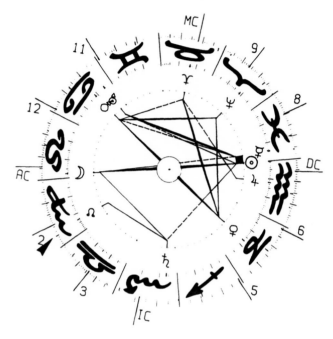

Chart 5. Hedwig Courths-Mahler, writer. *February 2, 1867, 16:45, Nebra, Germany. Koch houses. Using Lois M. Rodden's method of classification, this birth data is presented as "C" data.*

In which case, one must start to create this sense of security by continuing to build up one's resources.

The area of life concerned is one in which, over a fairly long period in early youth, substantial acquisitions are being made. It does not matter if these are material, intellectual, or spiritual, provided they are solid. Then comes a second period, in which these solid values are put to work. Here, too, the key question is that of generosity—of whether or not one is prepared to give. If so, the discovery is made that abundant giving yields an abundant return.

When charts have this placement, one sometimes finds a poor self-image, especially when the Node receives green or red aspects.

The native underestimates his or her personal merit, which, in the 2nd house, is judged by possessions. Consequently there can be a determination to hold on to these possessions without sharing them; also a desire to collect more. On the other hand, the native can become dependent on the wealth of others.

With the Node in the 2nd house, the vital assets are sound, but this fact is left out of account until it registers in the conscious mind. The complaint is made that one is being exploited, or that others are earning more or are better off than oneself. But when the influence of the Moon's Node enters consciousness, it brings with it a belief in one's intrinsic worth.

The Node in the 3rd house

The first two houses are still very much involved with the "I." In the 3rd house we enter the collective sphere, and our attitude to the group is important. In order to pick up the thoughts of the group (i.e., of those who are in my own thoughts), I must listen to, and understand, the language they are using. I must make my unconscious states of dependence conscious and, above all, I must be aware of my tendency to tell people what they want to hear. See Chart 6 for an example placement.

Inherently, the collective sphere is always a problem in the horoscope, because it is too close to us. Our reactions to the group, whether in thought (3rd house) or feeling (4th house) are completely automatic; as, for example, when I say something on the spur of the moment which, although it flatters the other person, is not absolutely true. And, with the Node in the 3rd house, we need to guard our tongues, because speech is the means of communication there. At least we should go over what we have said and consider whether or not we were right to advocate it, and whether or not it is objectively true. Possibly we have agreed with someone simply to please them or to avoid an argument.

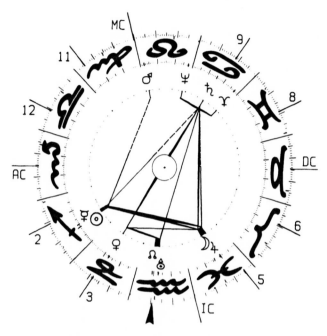

Chart 6. Curd Jürgens, actor. *December 13, 1915, 05:00 Central European time, Munich, Germany. Koch houses. Birth data: from birth certificate ("A" data from Gauquelin).*

If we make it a rule to check what we say, we can come to terms fairly quickly with our Node—something that is very important when there is an opposition to the Node. Naturally, we have to talk in the same way as everybody else, but we must do so with common sense and avoid exaggeration. In other words, we must use contemporary ideas and thought structures but with discrimination. Only then can we find our true niche, and avoid being pigeon-holed. The individual has to conform within reason, but the group has no right to demand submission. On the other hand, the individual is not entitled to expect submission from the group. There is a world of difference between heedlessly allowing oneself

to be controlled by others, and seeing how far one can accommo-
date them after making up one's own mind via the 9th house. The
need to do the latter is indicated by the placement of the Node in
the 3rd house.

The Node in the 4th House

In the 4th house, emotional values are all-important. It is not
enough, as in the 3rd house, simply to inquire about the meaning of something; one must be able to enter into it with feeling.
With the Node here, we are like a bird that felt good in its cosy
nest and was thrown out of it. Usually the chart will exhibit a tendency on the part of the native to lack balance and to be over-
eager to stress his or her own individuality. The lesson to learn is
to be an ordinary human being among other human beings, and
to be able to give and take emotionally. See Chart 7 for an example placement.

Often the 4th-house Node is counterbalanced by the Sun,
Uranus, or Pluto at the top of the chart; and this produces, by
reflex action, the wish to be famous or a leader. When emotional
imaginative pictures to do with the family or the group enter consciousness, these guiding images have to be clarified.

If planets in the 9th or 10th house show high ambition, this
can be satisfied; but, with the Node in the 4th house, the native
needs to keep close to home and roots. The feet need to be kept
firmly on the ground. Bottlenecks, which hold up progress, are
often encountered. Now, when blockages occur, the native's reaction is to try and forge ahead. In many cases, that would be the
right thing to do, but with the Moon's Node in the 4th house, it is
wrong. The proper course of action is to pull back and to live as one
of the group, as one of the family. This is the only way to prepare to
move forward again, to find room for maneuver, to gain access to
those it is desired to lead. Then misunderstandings will be swept
away and a fresh impetus will be given to upward development.

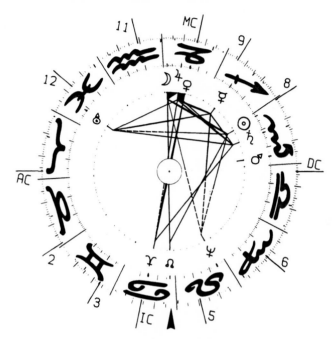

Chart 7. Robert F. Kennedy, politician. *November 20, 1925, 14:48, Brookline, MA. Koch houses. Data given to us by Kennedy's office in 1967.*

With Nodes in the 4th house that receive red aspects, there can be a retreat into a pleasant ideal world of acceptance and domestic bliss. This "warm nest" feeling has a very important function. It is one of the fundamentals of life, and we may well want to experience it at all costs. This makes us undifferentiated and dependent on the activities of the family. We are governed by these activities, and do not have a hand in shaping them but are sacrificed to the family's interests. In the worst scenario, our relatives assume the right to abuse us and to walk all over us.

When there is a planet in the 10th house, in opposition to the Node, the native will readily part with a place in the nest in order, at least, to make sure of getting on in the world. Ambition, in whatever form it occurs, destroys the sense of domesticity. The natural need to be part of a bigger organism, group, or family, comes off second best.

With a square from a planet on the Ascendant, the departure from normal is not excessive, but the native is too egotistic; with a square from the Descendent, the native defers to the partner. If, for the sake of personal development, the need to belong is allowed to wither, an essential human quality dies, and the individual becomes a loner and inclined to do wrong to others. For the ability to avoid unfairness is based on the nest-like environment of the 4th house.

The Node in the 5th House

In the 5th house, we are concerned with proving ourselves or presenting ourselves, in a direct way, to the "You." We must learn to face everyone openly and fearlessly, and must be capable of somehow drawing attention to ourselves as individuals. The 5th house is one of the three houses which have to do, in the most intense and direct way, with self-presentation and self-promotion. The most apt description of the 5th house is that it signifies the development of "presence," to be self-assured and not easily put off by a critical word or a short retort, to be able to persuade others by our confident bearing and by the strength of our personality. These are prominent features of this placement of the Node. See Chart 8 for an example placement.

Eroticism also belongs to the 5th house, but the mistake is often made of confusing eroticism with sexual appetite. Sex can be one of its functions, but sexuality occurs in all the houses, although admittedly in different forms and connections. In itself, eroticism is not sexual, but rather emotional or sensorial attraction that may function also among people of the same sex as friendship or Platonic love. It is the direct, vital connection

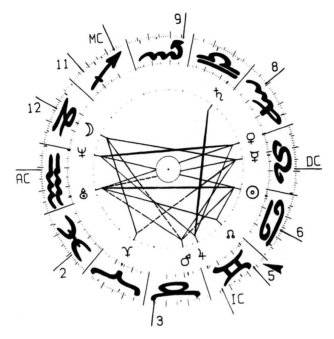

Chart 8. Edgar Degas, French painter. *July 19, 1834, 20:30 LT, Paris, France. Koch houses. Birth data from birth certificate (Gauquelin).*

between one human being and another. It is felt as a tingling and excitement when in the neighborhood of a certain person. This is not unconditionally sexual. The purpose of eroticism is to put one in touch with others by means other than conversation.

With the Node in the 5th house, the native has to seek closeness to others, a closeness that is stimulating and conveys a permanent sense of warmth. In this respect, eroticism can be incredibly fine, cultivated, and elevated. Physically, it is tactile and involves entering the field of vibration of another and experiencing the interaction of one's own vibrational field with it. Of course, this can also operate in the sexual area, where the erotic is a primary impulse. The Node in the 5th house requires us to be straightforward and direct: then the other person will respond to us and our influence, and we shall have vital encounters. The 5th house is a fire house; so, inevitably, the encounters it promotes are vital.

Inhibitions are natural; but, with this placement of the Node, it is very important that we do not allow ourselves to be overcome by our situation, but that we remain ourselves. Otherwise this pole, which is one that specifically represents us, can no longer exist as part of a dual or multiple erotic field of vibration, but is overwhelmed. Thus the Moon's Node requires us to be active and strong in a relationship.

Therefore we must be ready to experiment, and to take risks. When we make contact with a person and feel these vibrations, we do not know what will come of it. We may decide to stay as we are for the most part. Then, in principle, nothing negative can occur, and we shall harm no one. The concentration is at the "I," the "You" reacts to it, and the "I" is strengthened by meeting a strong "I": both of them sharpen their identities and profit from the encounter.

The Node in the 6th House

Here our problems are existential, and we are concerned with maintaining ourselves—unlike the situation in the 5th house, where we simply stand and make our presence felt and where being is more important than doing. However, even the 6th house is not primarily concerned with doing, but with gaining a clear idea of what one is capable of doing. See Chart 9 for an example placement.

The 6th house is a mutable [technically speaking, a cadent] house, and mutable houses always have to do with realization. It employs the process of realization to find its own "untapped market." It prompts us to ask, "Where are abilities like mine in demand, where am I needed, where would I fit in?" The question may appear to be academic, but it is real enough; for a 6th house

Chart 9. Alan Leo, astrologer and author. *August 7, 1860, 05:49, West-minster, England. Koch houses. Birth data from Leo's journal,* The Astrologer, *February 1890.*

presupposes a 5th, i.e., it presupposes that we already possess 5th-house self-assurance and enjoy a certain status.

In the 6th house we are concerned with being able to make proper use of the I that has been put to the test in the 5th house. Thus we are concerned with becoming part of the environment, and with making a personal contribution to it, while earning a living at the same time. Basically, in the 6th house—especially if the Node is posited there—we should look on ourselves as a supplier who can satisfy a demand, saying, "I wish to make a contribution to my local community. Now where is this contribution required?" It is a question of putting others first, because the 6th house is a house of service.

The principle of service should be recognized as a valid principle. Leo rules, and Virgo serves, but their roles can be seen in reverse, as when it is said of a king that he is the chief servant of his people. Similarly, the 6th house does not necessitate servility, or passive, compliant acceptance. It calls for a positive contribution, provided our contribution meets a real need; for this is what service is all about. Often we have to do hard work, and make an effort that taxes our strength and may even seem to be bad for us; but, with the Node in the 6th house, such experiences are a necessary part of life. We can grit our teeth and say, "I know this is no good to me. Nevertheless, I will do it, because the situation calls for it." If we are harboring some illusion about our abilities, the Node in the 6th house will undeceive us, and will show us the truth about what we can and cannot do.

In the 6th house it is important to perform, as briskly and as cheerfully as possible, the task that lies to hand. We need to resist the temptation (held out to us by the Neptunian 12th house) to sit and dream. Success in the 6th house comes by tackling a job oneself, without waiting for someone else to do it. One should do one's best, even if the task seems to be beneath one's dignity, or leaves us feeling that we always have to do everything ourselves. Because it is by our personal participation that everything gets under way and is organized. The whole secret of the 6th house lies in the continual fulfillment of obligations, and in a wholehearted application of one's abilities to achieve common goals.

The Node in the 7th House

This house is opposite the 1st, so things go into reverse. What was negative with the Descending Node is now positive with the Ascending Node. The 7th house is one for making contacts and agreements; but care must be taken that the agreements are mutual. The terms of a contract, for example, must be observed by both parties, and each party should derive some benefit from it. We find the Node in the 7th house in individuals of two types. Firstly, we find it in those who are egocentric and think that everything should revolve round themselves. Such people never make proper contacts or enter into genuine partnerships. Secondly, we find it in those who are not forceful enough to assert, "I want my share." Usually such people try to justify themselves by a show of ethics, saying, "It is wrong to be mercenary; we should give without expecting anything in return. We ought not to look for praise after doing a good deed, nor should we take money for spiritual work." See Chart 10, below, for an example placement.

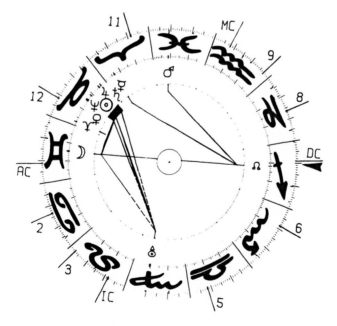

Chart 10. Pierre Teilhard de Chardin, philosopher. *May 1, 1881, 07:00 LT, Orcines, Clermont, France. Koch houses. Birth data: birth certificate, "A" data from Gauquelin.*

There has to be give and take in the 7th house. It corresponds to the sign Libra, the Scales, the balance of accounts between the "You" and the "I." The presence of the Node in the 7th house means that we must keep striking a balance between ourselves and others. In the main, it serves to hold our fits of egotism in check. We must make sure that our agreements are fair to both sides, and must check them objectively. The 7th house is an air house, and the air temperament is given to thought and is not entirely wrapped up in emotion.

When the Moon's Node is in the 7th house, this can mean that we are not keen on commitment or that we are unduly nervous of provisos. Therefore we must learn to enter into permanent relationships. These will have certain consequences: they will bind us, impose obligations on us, and limit our personal freedom. Also, in our development, the tie to a partner draws us in a certain direction or limits our range of movement. But whole-hearted commitment is perfectly natural, and it is important to cultivate a willingness to enter into valid relationships. These involve natural duties and restrictions; which may, in time, be felt as a deprivation of liberty; which is why there is often a reluctance to seek such commitments.

With the Node in the 7th house, the idea is to moderate one's characteristics and self-absorption in order to leave the other party to the contract equal scope for self-expression. They deserve the same rights and benefits as we have and the same degree of freedom to be themselves. The keywords of the Node in the 7th house are reciprocity and equilibrium. As a regulatory feature, we often find the Node in the 7th house accompanied by many planets on the Ascendent to balance the egocentricity. When there are conflicts within the partnership, we can restore the status quo by opening up and recognizing that it is up to us to make the first move. With the Node in the 7th house, the "I" is afraid to trust, or to accept help from, the "You." The "I" must overcome its fear and hesitation and be prepared for commitment.

In the 7th house, we have access to the Whole in an active creative process via the "You," just as in the 4th house we have access to the Group. In being responsible for the "You," in dedicating ourselves to others, further development takes place, even when the aspects in the horoscope do not favor partnership. With the Node in the 7th house, partnership is a learning process that has to be accepted. Frequently we have to do things for our development which the horoscope negates elsewhere.

The Node in the 8th House

The 8th house lies halfway between the Descendant (DC) and the Medium Coeli or Midheaven (MC). Like the other fixed houses, it has no contact with the main axes. Like them, it is relatively remote from the cardinal force and favors a settled state of affairs. A dual instinct resides in the Scorpio 8th house. It rules the situation in which two things are wanted at the same time: the thing that suits the Descendant, and the thing that suits the Medium Coeli. Both of the nearer main axes determine the themes of the fixed houses. See Chart 11, page 62, for an example placement.

This produces a double nature. In the 8th house there is a desire to fulfill two conditions: On the one hand, to be in good communication with the "You," and to profit by the contacts made through the 7th house; on the other hand, to undergo a 10th house individualization. However, to stress one's individuality can lead to isolation and to the loss of advantages offered by the 7th house. To be entirely "Me," I have to give up "You." Therefore, I am torn between two desires. Although I want optimum access to those around me, I also want to be a strong, independent, free individual. And so I seek to be someone important in society. That is a classic compromise which society has always found acceptable.

Society is the sum of all the "You's," and if I climb the social ladder and reach a secure position, I become someone who is respected. But, conversely, when I have a social position, I am answerable to others. To be sure, I have a place in society and

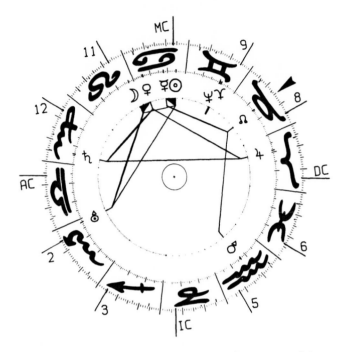

Chart 11. Pearl S. Buck, novelist. *June 26, 1892, 12:30 EST, Hillsboro, WV. Koch houses. Birth data from Lois M. Rodden's* Profiles of Women *(Tempe, AZ: American Federation of Astrologers, 1979) p. 102.*

authorization to perform a certain function, but, equally, I am under society's eye.

The Node in the 8th house warns me that I need to understand these two conflicting requirements, and to handle them sensibly without making false compromises. In fact any compromise is rather inconclusive. With the Node in the 8th house, I am compelled to live on the razor's edge. I must guard against opting for security at the cost of personal development.

In the 8th house, the Node challenges us to strike a proper balance between society and individual growth: a balance that will produce spiritual and personal harmony. It requires us to cultivate a healthy relationship with the environment, in which the latter is respected, and to fulfill our obligations without hindrance to our spiritual growth. This is a tall order, because it presumes an internal and an external independence that are not easy to come by. It implies give and take in the spirit of: "Render unto Caesar the things that are Caesar's . . . " Not by seizing advantages, but by giving and taking in such a way that we and others each get what is our due. It is important to keep things in proportion, and to do so calls for the ability to keep a cool head and to weigh everything carefully; also to be scrupulous in keeping the rules, including the rules of affection, sympathy and contact.

Also one must not neglect love while getting on in the world. In the 8th house there has to be equilibrium between the physical and the spiritual. One is constantly being challenged not to lay undue emphasis on status or on material advantage. Usually, when the Node is in the 8th house, there is a struggle to overcome a fixation on the tangible and material, and to release living human impulses.

The Node in the 9th House

The 9th house has to do with the development of individual thought, or spiritual autonomy. What is involved here is the 3–9 (or thought) axis. In the 3rd house, our task is to learn the language, and to absorb the knowledge, of the group. In childhood, we accept the thought-structures of our environment, of the group in which we live, and we are molded by the thinking of those around. The collective enshrines not only knowledge but also routine patterns of thought which are almost mechanical. Thinking in the 3rd house is fairly reflex and travels along fixed lines. See Chart 12, page 64, for an example placement.

In the 9th house, there is an awareness of, and an ability to distinguish, those thought-structures and routines, those scripts or

Chart 12. Georges Braque, French painter. *May 9, 1882, 02:30 LT, Paris Argenteuil, France. Koch houses. Birth data: birth certificate, "A" data from Gauquelin.*

programs, which have become second nature. And not until this state of awareness is reached can we discard the things that do not tally with what we have worked out for ourselves. In the 9th house we must create our own philosophy of life and strive for intellectual freedom. We must form a picture of the world that is as objective and as devoid of value-judgments as possible; by examining things for ourselves, making up our minds about them, and so arriving at our own outlook on life. The evidence of our senses should provide food for thought. The ability to draw conclusions from what is observed, to follow the course of events, and to have clear ideas and a personal point of view, is typical of the 9th house. Our prerequisites are accurate observations and keen perceptions, from which valid results can be obtained, inferences made, and our own attitude developed. Muddled ideas carried over from the 3rd house can be full of prejudice, however, and may make it difficult to think clearly in the 9th house.

Therefore, with the Node in the 9th house, we need to make a special effort to form own opinions and to draw up a clear account of them. We should try to avoid being led astray by others either intentionally or unintentionally, or by automatic responses of our own that spoil clarity and obstruct freedom of thought. If we come across a good idea, it is not good because it is said to be good, or because it emanates from some authority; it is good only if we can verify it by obtaining the same results. Verification is the task of the 9th house.

Keen senses are absolutely vital for clear thought. Keen senses are symbolized by Jupiter, the ruler of Sagittarius, which is the counterpart of the 9th house. Obviously, there is a connection between observation and thought, and this connection is represented by the 9th house (and by Sagittarius). Our senses need to be in good working order before we can make clear judgments.

We require the courage of our convictions when putting forward our own ideas. We need to be self-confident to trust our own observations and feelings and not to be persuaded by the crowd that we have seen, or should see, something different. The 9th house encourages us to stick to our point of view, and to the truth we have discovered for ourselves. Of course, we must not think that we are always right or that we can do anything. The progress indicated by the Node in the 9th house comes about through expanded awareness by means of original thinking, traveling, and philosophizing, etc., after we have left the route charted for us by others. When we take an independent line, query what we are told, and experience things for ourselves, we learn what life really is.

The Node in the 10th House

With the Node in the 10th house, the important thing is to develop our own individuality and, out of the possibilities that lie before us, choose those that promote self-knowledge. Self-knowledge is different from outward self-awareness. The latter would hinder rather than help our development as an individual. In rising to the challenge of the Node in the 10th house, we must run our own life and cast off the leading-strings of others. This task is as hard as that of the 8th house, because we perch on the razor's edge and are always depending on someone, or are always being criticized and judged by the group. See Chart 13 for an example placement.

In the 10th house, illusions of grandeur nearly always occur. These cover the whole range: authority, eminence, success and power. Prestige is not the main consideration, because that is an 8th house matter. Prestige is a concept based on possessions, not on authority. Therefore, in the 10th house, either one has natural authority or one puts on a show of it, i.e., one usurps authority. The latter is mere role-playing, and ties in with the fact that Saturn, the master of forms, rules the 10th house. But such role-playing cannot replace authority.

The 10th house is also the house of vocation, and we need to set our sights on a vocation rather than on fame. In a vocation, we undertake for the group some assignment that confronts us. The mature person feels called upon to do something for the group; he or she becomes involved in it, and achieves goals that serve the community.

The 10th house is an earth house (Capricorn). The function of each house can be inferred from the relationship of the temperaments within a given triplicity. Thus Capricorn relates back to the activities of the Virgo house, just as the Virgo house relates back to the activities of the Taurus house. Because Taurus lies nearest to the beginning of the zodiac, its counterpart, the 2nd house, has priority; the 6th house is next in line, and finally we

Chart 13. Henri Rousseau, French painter. *May 21, 1844, 01:00 LT, Laval, France. Koch houses. Birth data: birth certificate, "A" data from Gauquelin.*

have the 10th house. The latter represents so-called social development, which can take place here.[1]

With the Node in the 10th house, it is necessary to forego traditional and family goals. A family attitude toward status and profession has been impressed on us; but we must break free from it in order to find our own guiding image and, so to speak, pack our bags and set out toward a destination of our own.

---

[1]See also Volume 3 in our *Lifeclock* series, published in English as *Astrology and the Spiritual Path* (York Beach, ME: Samuel Weiser, 1990).

It is especially hard for women to realize the promise of the Node in the 10th house in countries where they do not enjoy equal opportunities. In such circumstances, in order to make good themselves, they often enter into partnership with some man who is rising in the world. However, this is a temporary role, a part they often play brilliantly without making real progress. If the partnership runs into trouble, the woman may be left to shift for herself; often she will have to abandon an easy life in order to achieve individuation. In this way she learns to stand on her own two feet and to gain authority, and she makes her mark as an individual in her own right.

The Node in the 10th house demands self-determination, independent decision-making, and development of a resolute will. Self-discipline is also required, because there is a natural 4th-house inclination to merge with the group. With the Node in the 10th house, it is important to pursue one's own individuation consistently (as per C. G. Jung) without paying any attention to criticism.

The price of developing an independent personality is a certain degree of isolation and loneliness. Paying it prevents us from scrambling to success on the backs of others.

The Node in the 11th House

The 11th house belongs to the axis of relationships. Like the 5th house, it has to do with the attitudes and behavior of people to one another. In the 5th house, human relationships are tackled with a naïve simplicity. One sees oneself as the center of the world and tries to realize personal desires or ideals. In the 11th house, this self-oriented view has to be abandoned. Its simplistic methods will no longer work, because one recognizes that one is part of a Whole. Here one must act, on principle, in accordance with transcendent, universal criteria. Postulating these criteria is even more important than working hard on them. See Chart 14, page 69, for an example placement.

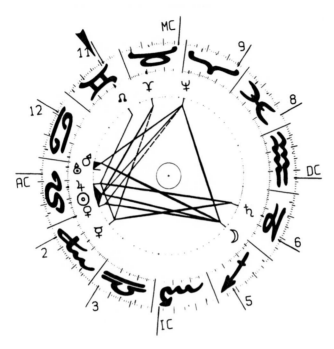

Chart 14. Sri Aurobindo, integral yoga. *May 18, 1872, 04:30 LT, Calcutta, India. Koch houses. (Birth data from* Auraville-Stadtder Zukunftsmenchen, *Stuttgart: Fischer).*

When the Node is in the 11th house, it is important to establish a clear attitude toward people. This can be personal, for in a personal sense the 11th house is known as the house of friendship. It represents the possession of friends and confidant(e)s. It represents making a choice of people who have a certain quality, in which there always resides an element of trust. This element of trust clearly divides the 11th house from the 5th. On a personal level, the Node in the 11th house indicates a need to form friendships and to make the most of them. We have to learn to be selective when looking for friends and to seek kindred spirits who will turn out to be genuine. We may be parted from such friends for years but when we meet them again it is as if we had been with them only yesterday. That is true friendship. In the 11th house the discovery can be made, as soon as we learn to stop clinging, that loyal devotion is possible even without conditions. Then complete freedom of action is granted in the friendship. What this means is that with the Node in the 11th house, we must overcome the desire for security characteristic of the Fixed Cross, and put it behind us.

In essence, friendship is the result of striving for an ethical attitude to others. From this point of view, the 11th house aims at the development of an ideal concept of humanity. Basically, what is meant here by ethics is mutual respect between individuals. Although we work at this (or discover it) in the 9th house, ethics is a fundamental frame of reference in the 11th house. Naturally, it is a frame of reference for doctrines and creeds; for the 11th is a fixed house and, in a fixed house, conditions rather than processes hold sway. Therefore, the ethics with which the 11th house is concerned are ready-made ethics, in which one believes, or with which one identifies sufficiently strongly to want to pass them on to others or even to impose them on them. Dogmatism almost always emanates from the 11th house, which has to do with our convictions and our moral yardstick.

In the Node receives red aspects, there is a likelihood of blind acceptance of a certain ethical view. Even a sophisticated and complex system of ethics can be passively absorbed—usually as a result of the upbringing or of social influences in youth, chiefly at the time of puberty.

Green aspects to the Node should be heeded, too, because they introduce an element of uncertainty. When they are present, we are susceptible to any number of ideologies that promise security. This can lead to difficulties, especially in the practical arena of friendship, because we are prepared to change our friends whenever we change our ethical beliefs.

When blue aspects are received by the Node, or by a planetary stellium, there is often an inclination to join an elite group or to embrace a special doctrine because this seems to be the most convenient thing to do. We cradle ourselves in the security of the group, and use it for our own ends. And so we need to make an effort to overcome what is indicated by the Node here. For a start, we should examine our ethics. In the 11th house, and with blue aspects, this is not particularly easy, because our ethics are second nature to us. We may change our opinions but, unconsciously, we react according to ingrained patterns of behavior.

So, with the Node in the 11th house, we ought to take pains to acquire a satisfactory system of ethics that is clearly formulated and intelligently accepted. Otherwise we may indulge in spiritual snobbery, and pretensions to exceptional moral virtue. Egocentricity in ethics produces the smugness that says: "I am better than others, because I know how to behave," or, "We are better than others, because we know how to behave."

The Node in the 11th house serves notice that we ought to take responsibility for our own actions and ought not to rely on others. Doing the latter is a big danger, because solidarity with the group gives us a feeling of strength, and we imagine we are entitled by some dogma or ethical system to sit in judgment on people and call them mistaken or wicked. Behind the group-egoism involved in special friendships there lurks an individual egoism, though we may hide it under a shiny white cloak of ethics.

The Node in the 12th House

The 12th house is the one furthest removed form the outside world. It is well away from the "You"-point. In addition, it is a very introvert house and corresponds to the passive sign of Pisces. The native waits for someone with initiative to make a move. It is the place of turning inward and of self-discovery. The Node in the 12th house means that this person needs, from time to time, to withdraw from active life for the purpose of self-remembering. See Chart 15, page 72, for an example placement.

The 1st and 12th houses form the "I"-space in the house system; and sandwiched between them is the "I"-point, the Ascen-

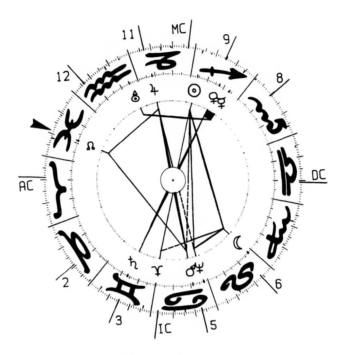

Chart 15. Willy Brandt, politician. December 18, 1913, 12:45 Central European Time, Lübeck, Germany. Koch houses. Birth data: birth certificate, "A" data from Gauquelin.

dant. In the 1st house the "I" is extravert: it faces the world and announces: "Here I am!" The introvert "I"-house is the 12th house. Here we do not exhibit ourselves to the world; but keep some space between it and us for the sake of being wholly ourselves. Being ourselves implies knowing and accepting ourselves for the one we really are. Self-observation, self-knowledge, and self-discovery are tasks to be undertaken here.

In addition, there is something greater and more pivotal we can do. We can discover our membership of the greater, or cosmic Whole, our relationship to humanity, and to God. This transcendental experience enables us to feel woven into an all-embracing

Reality. Even though we are separate individuals, we are nevertheless parts of a macrocosm, the whole of creation. We do not perceive this in its unimaginable wealth of details, but can experience it as a unity.

The individual would not survive without being part of a whole. Incorporation of the self in a greater Whole is the object of the 12th house, and the Moon's Node here invites us to make that object our aim. Union with reality, which it can help us to attain, is the best and surest source of health.

There is no substitute for the basic confidence provided by discernment in the 12th house. It gives an awareness of infinite being in which all things are contained. Here, too, is the area of religion, where the experience of God transcends theory. And it includes the religious experience of someone who does not have a religion but is occupied (for example) with the cosmos as the infinite totality of space, and has much the same experience as a believer, although understanding it differently.

Anyone who has this position of the Node must learn not to regard abstract ideas as real entities. The place for these is the 6th house, which is the depository of those 12th-house creations that are useful for everyday life. But this experience of an infinity in which everything is contained, this experience of God or the Cosmos as a vast expanse, cannot be put into words; for in the 12th house we leave behind the area of the imaginable. (See figure 6 on page 74.) Indeed, only by doing so can we have a genuine, deep, and all-embracing experience. Yet, because of its character, the experience is strange and unsettling, since all categories of thought, feeling, and doing, are abandoned. On catching sight of this expanse, we are afraid of disintegrating, or of falling uncontrollably into a yawning abyss. It is a leap into nothingness, and resembles death.

We need to understand the Node in the 12th house in such a way that we are able, from time to time, to retire into this space that belongs to all created beings in the universe and yet is completely individual to us. We can learn to withdraw into ourselves; far enough, indeed, to become the Whole again. We can learn to

Figure 6. Sol et ejus umbra *[The Sun and its shadow]. The Earth between light and darkness. (Michael Maier,* Scrutinum Chymicum, *Frankfurt, 1687.)*

pray, meditate, and contemplate, and may be awestruck by discovering a great sublimity. Each of us will do this in his or her own way: one goes to church, another contemplates the starry sky. Getting results does not depend on the objective space with which one identifies, or on a given place, but depends on the capacity and the will to expand and direct one's awareness.

Chapter 4

The Moon's Node in the Signs

The Difference between Houses and Zodiac Signs • The Node in Aries • The Node in Taurus • The Node in Gemini • The Node in Cancer • The Node in Leo • The Node in Virgo • The Node in Libra • The Node in Scorpio • The Node in Sagittarius • The Node in Capricorn • The Node in Aquarius • The Node in Pisces •

The Difference between Houses and Zodiac Signs

The signs of the zodiac are twelve equal divisions of the ecliptic (the apparent circular path of the Sun through the heavens), and each measures thirty degrees. They form a cosmic reference system enabling us to survey the course of the year. The zodiac is part of our cosmic space (the solar system) and influences the whole earth. Thus the signs may be seen as cosmic qualities, as energy sources available to everybody. From the point of view of astropsychology, the signs represent what we bring with us into the world, our hereditary disposition or genetic structure. The houses, on the other hand, divide the terrestrial space surrounding the native into twelve fields, and therefore possess an individual and local character: they show our relationship to our actual environment. See figure 7 on page 76.

Whereas the Node in a particular house indicates the area of life in which the first step towards further development should be taken, the Node in a zodiac sign supplies information as to the motivating qualities or intentions that are already present. The time taken by the Moon's Node to travel through the entire zodiac is 18 years, 7 months and 10 days. On average, the Node remains in a sign for 1-1/2 years. In the zodiac, too, the placement of the Node can be instructive and helpful.

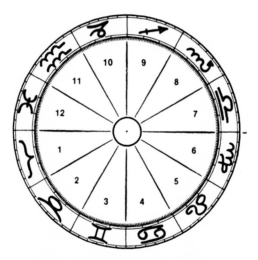

Aries	1st house	Libra	7th house
Taurus	2nd house	Scorpio	8th house
Gemini	3rd house	Sagittarius	9th house
Cancer	4th house	Capricorn	10th house
Leo	5th house	Aquarius	11th house
Virgo	6th house	Pisces	12th house

Figure 7. The signs and houses.

The Node in Aries

Aries is the cardinal fire sign. It is "the" sign par excellence, in which self-manifestation takes place. Here, the "I" must stand out against the world, and especially against the "You." We must be able to say "Yes" to ourselves, and to express this attitude in our lifestyle. Nevertheless, the way in which the desire for self-assertion is expressed by the Aries native will depend on our state of awareness. Or, to put it another way, the hazier the picture we have of ourselves, the more we resort to force, but the more differentiated our consciousness is, the more subtly we proceed. Yet even when being fairly subtle we still use "push"—we have plenty of that. The "I" tends to manifest itself in what may be pictured as a series of pulsations. The same is true when the Moon's Node is in Aries: we try to bring our personality to bear on the world in order to make things happen. This placement of the Node is usually a fairly strong incentive to be creative. Someone with the Node in Aries is incapable of settling down to routine work, even when output would increase. Increased output is not a consideration with Aries; what matters is creating something unlike anything anyone else can create. To produce something creative that is completely personal is the ultimate in self-expression for this sign.

With red aspects to the Node, there is a danger of over-producing like some sort of "Stakhanovite." The native engages in hectic activity, and revels in quantity instead of being creative. However, the individual with the Node in Aries can produce an enormous amount of truly creative work.

The Node in Taurus

The fixed earth sign, Taurus, follows Aries and therefore its task is connected with what Aries does. Creative work adds to one's resources, and increases the available capital.

Now in Taurus the task is to administer, to turn to account, and to use one's resources. One must not use other people's resources—that is something Scorpio can do, but not Taurus, because Taurus is on the left-hand or "I"-side of the chart, and Scorpio is on the right-hand or "You"-side.

In the "I"-region of the zodiac, our own assets rather than those of others are in play. It can lead to difficulties if Taurus tries to exploit the capital of others. This is a particular danger when the Node receives red aspects.

Therefore it is important to turn our talents, abilities, and knowledge to account, and to place them at the disposal of others while still making use of them ourselves. Naturally, care must be taken to provide our own resources in the first place. Also, with the Node in Taurus, the task is to add to our assets, and to replenish them if necessary. If we simply draw on them—as it is so easy to do under red aspects—eventually we shall have nothing left. Then we shall lie back unable to do anything further, because our energy is more or less spent. The native with the Node in Taurus must ensure this does not happen.

The Taurean is a very clever negotiator, and has an extremely economical outlook. He or she immediately discovers weak points and is always intent on removing any imbalance that might lead to overspending. Steps are taken straight away to restore stability.

When the Node is in Taurus, we should husband our resources so as to avoid wasting our vital energies. The placement can also be an indication that we should look after our health, seeing that health is an essential part of our personal assets.

The Node in Gemini

Aries expends its energies on the world as a matter of course, without considering whether they are wanted or not. Taurus uses its energies economically and to best advantage, but is still extravagant in the sense that the world is not given the choice of rejecting what is being offered.

On the other hand, the mutable air sign, Gemini, is very intent on interacting with the environment. This interaction is important for Gemini, which needs to give and take, and is happy only when conveying ideas and forming relationships.

Gemini natives are invariably caught up in what is going on around them; there is a continual energy exchange between them and the world. With the Node in Gemini, we have to pass on our gains. Our relationships are a network through which we receive what we want to know and give back what we have learned.

This is the basic characteristic of Gemini. Connections have to be made and maintained to allow a continual energy flow back and forth. Such activities are a constant preoccupation. Gemini is typically mutable, and is happy to share its knowledge and know-how; at the same time, it is eager to take advantage of what the world knows, has, and is able to do.

Thus the Gemini Node can show there is much of immediate value for us to learn from those around us. This means keeping in touch with the world physically, mentally, and spiritually, in a lively but intelligent way. It means that we do not avoid people but try to have permanent points of contact with them.

The Node in Cancer

Manifestation processes come to the fore again in the cardinal sign Cancer. In its manifestation, Cancer is oriented toward the collective as a whole. The native wants access to a home or "nest." He or she needs to be part of a family and hates to be alone. Group membership gives a sense of protection and warmth. If the Node is in Cancer, the individual should try to join in. Very often, a Node with this placement occurs in strong-minded individuals who are much inclined to do their own thing and to withdraw from the crowd. In the extreme case, they live like hermits because they believe they are better or more exalted than others.

The Node in a collective sign indicates that one should become involved in a collective, in order to feel part of a family, group, local community, nation, or the whole human race. The native could become the center of a hive perhaps. For this a measure of industry and activity is required—as befits a cardinal sign. People with the Node in Cancer cannot laze about and do nothing; they must become involved in the creation of a collective relationship for their own benefit, and preferably for the benefit of others also.

The easiest way for them to do this is to found a family. With the Node in Cancer it is important to be able to achieve emotional harmony with those around. Any tendency toward solitude and isolation opposes this placement of the Node. The emotional experience of community and belonging has a big role to play here.

The Node in Leo

In the fixed sign Leo, we are concerned with gaining a secure position in life. Leo is also a fire sign, and the Leo personality consumes for its own benefit the living space surrounding others. Leo wants to be a monarch, and to possess a realm of which it can be said: "Here I am at home, and here I will carry out my activities. This is my territory, and I will never surrender it." Leo always keeps a firm grip on a personal world that represents security in the changing scenes of life; and, of course, people play a decisive part in these scenes.

With the Node in Leo we should adopt a positive, well-defined attitude to our environment. We ought to make ourselves known, place ourselves in the center of our world, and learn to cope with it. Usually the world does not leave us alone but is continually provoking confrontations. Anyway, this position of the Node helps to correct our development, and brings us out into the open.

In charts indicating a certain hesitancy or nervousness over making one's presence felt, a Node with this placement may help to overcome this tendency. The Node here encourages the individual to come out of his or her shell and be willing to take a few risks. Finally, this Node urges us to test ourselves in the world, and be willing to experience euphoric self-realization, the suffering of reverses, along with everything that lies in between. As a Leo, we may seem to ourselves and others to be very much on the offensive all the time; in reality, however, we are very much on the defensive; for Leo is a fixed sign, and only the fire in it produces the touch of aggression.

The Node in Virgo

The mutable, earth sign, Virgo, calls for mobility, fluidity, and flexibility. In contrast to Leo, we should total up everything of real value in our life, and discard the pomp and circumstance. We must come to terms with the community in which we live and with the environment as a whole. The "You" is clearly emphasized here.

Leo also lays emphasis on the "You," but in Leo we are free to make an impression on the world. Virgo is a serving sign, in which we are in a weak position and more or less at the mercy of others. Society has the last word, and our partner tells us what to do. When the Node is in Virgo, we even have to let the world decide what good we are and assign us a place—not the place we may dream of occupying, but the one for which we are suited. Conformity and adaptability are keynotes of Virgo. Now, to have to knuckle under can be very tiresome, not to mention painful. For this reason we find many Virgoans grumbling about the miserable circumstances they have had to endure.

Of course, a readiness to fit in and find one's proper place must not lead to identity loss—as can happen with red aspects to the Node. Then one would end up in a state of alienation and become nothing and nobody.

The Node in Virgo should make us willing to adopt a positive approach to the people around us, and to see and understand what they really need before giving them what we have to offer. In the Virgoan Node, helping and serving are essential forms of expression of an active and practical love for others.

The Node in Libra

The cardinal air sign, Libra, in contrast to Virgo, has a dynamic approach to the "You." We are able to react positively to the environment and to do something with it. We need not feel uneasy at making certain demands of the environment, but first we should ask the world, just as Virgo asks the world: "What can I do for you?" Then, on considering the reply, we can respond pleasantly. Our approach to society includes the attempt to come into harmony with it.

More especially, the native may wish to bring harmony to the world. Diplomacy can figure strongly in this placement of the Node—in the interests of concord of course. With red aspects, various compromises may be made in order to come out on top and look good at the same time. In the extreme case, the native says something to one person while saying the exact opposite to someone else.

With the Libran Node it is important to strike a balance between the "I" and the "You," to form a correct judgment, and to live in harmony with the world. For this a measure of self-discipline is required. The emotions have to be held in check if one is to avoid being thrown off balance and being carried away by private feelings and opinions. This position of the Node places a restraint on idiosyncrasy, excessive autonomy, and undue egocentricity.

The Node in Scorpio

In the fixed water sign, Scorpio, an effort is made to establish a regular system. Here, too, as in the opposite sign, Taurus, one is concerned with the use of material resources; now, however, they are other people's material resources. Thus in Scorpio we often meet the type that administers the property of others, manages them, utilizes and fosters their talents, and acts as an agent for their skills and services. In principle, the Scorpio Node challenges us to be prepared to act on behalf of others and to exploit their resources for their benefit and in accordance with their intentions. Obviously, in such a situation, the native has to stand back a little, though of course having a personal part to play. In order to exercise such a function they have to gain a place in society. The Scorpio Node always indicates an effort to achieve a certain social status. This can mean nothing more than ambition and the aspiration to be someone important; especially with red aspects to the Node. Scorpios always think they are able to decide what is good for others. Usually they can give them helpful advice on how to realize their assets, and on how to find the best chances of success.

Scorpios avail themselves of existing forms and structures. With the Scorpio Node, one can easily adapt to current social arrangements. One can also develop the knack of exploiting them to the advantage of oneself and others.

The Node in Sagittarius

The mutable fire sign, Sagittarius, and the cardinal earth sign, Capricorn, are the two individual signs that promote the expression and the maturation of the individual personality. In Sagittarius we always strive hard for mental autonomy. Sagittarians have an independent outlook. They want to work out their own ideas and philosophy and to have these under their own control. With the Node in Sagittarius, the task is to develop this mental autonomy.

One's thoughts should be fostered so as to produce clear-cut opinions of one's own and independence of the opinions of others.

This placement of the Node is quite likely to occur when the chart indicates that the native is very much inclined to fall in line with the opinions of others. In which case, its message is: "You must think for yourself and form your own views." This Node is an antidote to mental laziness.

With the Sagittarian Node, we have to answer for our opinions, which may not suit us at all, because we like to think that they are beyond criticism. In red-green aspects of the Node there is often a tendency to be dogmatic and fanatical.

In the fire sign Sagittarius, self-confidence becomes important again. The preceding fire signs, Aries and Leo, are brimming with self-confidence. However, matters are not quite so simple for Sagittarius, which has to prove, by its spiritual autonomy, that it has the right to stand up and be heard.

The Node in Capricorn

In the cardinal earth sign Capricorn, as in Sagittarius, a clear stand is taken in the world; but not in the sense of sustaining vigorous effort, as in Scorpio, or, as in Leo, of creating living space where one can rule like a king. Capricorn must establish its authority on a firm foundation. Ability gained by experience and hard work is what is required (earth sign). This firm foundation, laid with so much effort, must be placed at the disposal of others.

In Capricorn we have the true ruler who is able to lead others with genuine authority that may have taken a long time to develop. The masses follow Capricorn (whereas the group follows Cancer).

Capricorn, standing alone above the crowd, carries heavy responsibilities and must use its position and authority for the benefit of those who are lower down. The saying sometimes applied to Leo: "The king is the chief servant of his people" is easily shrugged off by Leo but does apply here. For Capricorn, ruling is not an end in itself but a function to be fulfilled for the good of those who are ruled, and it has to be earned by hard work.

So the Capricorn Node calls for competence, ability, skill, and knowledge. These things impart genuine authority and, as in Sagittarius, they entail accountability as well.

When the Node receives red aspects, and often when it receives blue-red aspects, the native may become a string-puller or gray eminence. There is a desire to exercise an influence behind the scenes without having to be made responsible.

The Node in Aquarius

In the fixed air sign, Aquarius, we are once more concerned with the establishment and maintenance of a position in life. In Aquarius, conscious attitudes in thought, ethics, and philosophy, come to the fore. Primary importance is attached to the rule of reason; practical living is secondary.

Aquarians know something about everything and revel in logical argument, in which a certain proposition may be deduced from given premises. In other words, they have a strong urge to view the world rationally and to work out a system by which things can be reshaped in everyday life. They tend to build castles in the air. If the Node receives a green aspect, for instance, Utopian plans are laid without reference to what may reasonably be achieved.

At their best, Aquarians strive to think clearly in order to see the world as it is. Because the Aquarian mind is mostly occupied with this world and with the social order, it looks for an unambiguous, usable form of ethics that offers solutions for contemporary problems. In that respect, Aquarius is like the previous fixed sign, Scorpio. The natives of both these signs are interested in creating an ideal system.

Now, in striving for a perfect social order, the first task is to keep order inside one's own head. With the Aquarian Node, the feelings often intervene and muddle the thoughts to some extent. Therefore order must first be established in the conscious mind, in the personal world of thought, before any crusading is done in the big world outside.

In the extreme case, there is a proneness to be dogmatic, and to admonish all and sundry who do not share one's ideals. This power-play is reminiscent of Leo; and, of course,the Descending Node is in Leo at the opposite pole of the axis.

The Node in Pisces

As the mutable water sign, Pisces is subject to a learning process, i.e., it is very important to be ready to learn. In Pisces, learning is not intellectual comprehension as in Gemini, nor is it practical as in Virgo, and it is not philosophical as in Sagittarius; it is an inner, existential learning on the spot, and has to do with the meaning of life.

This Node impels us to ask about the meaning of life whatever the answer may be. The answer will not remain the same all along: fresh truths will be discovered as we mature.

A red-aspected Node can indicate an attitude of sitting on the fence, which allows the native to jump either way. But, more usefully, the Pisces Node seeks a conscious way inward; it endeavors to deal with the world from a distance, expects nothing from the world, but tries to fathom its real meaning. Detachment is also sought in the transcendental sense: the development of individual consciousness beyond the normal confines in order to extend it into spiritual dimensions where the sense of being is deeper. In this way one's development can be furthered.

In Pisces, the native thinks and feels in cosmic dimensions, especially when meeting other people. The business of Pisces is to help, or rather to save. Now the saving done by Pisces differs from the practical help given by Virgo. Saving implies that the other person feels that his or her deepest motivations are understood. Saving means letting the other person know that his or her existence is recognized. Pisces is very good at this. Understanding the significance of the world and oneself as parts of the Whole, and saving others, is the highest task of the Piscean Node.

Chapter 5

The Moon-Node
Horoscope

The Moon's Node and the Inner Past • How is the Moon-Node
Horoscope Erected? • The Moon-Node Houses and their
Archetypal Definition • 1st through 12th Moon-Node
House • The Moon-Node Horoscope as Inner Capacity •

The Moon's Node and the Inner Past

Our next step is to penetrate the system as a whole, to descend into the depths of the Moon-Node system; which, so far, we know only as a way of approach to the superficial features of the horoscope describing the everyday character of the native.

In principle, we can understand the Moon-Node system from a psychological point of view. Psychology speaks of the shadow personality or the shadow function—defined differently by different psychological schools. This signifies something within that cannot be experienced directly and consciously. It dwells in a latent state in the depths of our being and is not easily accessed. We shall be looking at it more closely later, but for the moment we will just say that the shadow function can be pictured as a subliminal substratum where the deepest roots of our nature grow, and out of which various things rise from the dark unconscious during our lives. This layer is not get-at-able by ordinary psychological techniques, and many schools admit this, especially those belonging to C. G. Jung, Graf Durckheim, and others like them.

Now the beauty of the Moon-Node horoscope is that we can actually look inside the unconscious to see what slumbers there.

When this deep-seated structure is stirred up by an accident or by some circumstance in life, and breaks through to the surface in images or dreams, in sudden events or experiences, the usual reaction is a feeling that one is being assailed by an alien influence from outside that is beyond comprehension.

When, for example, we dream or daydream, we usually perceive it as something we ourselves are doing; on the other hand, we may decide that an external influence is at work. Something out of the ordinary seems to have entered our life; we are at a loss and cannot get our bearings. It is here that the Moon-Node horoscope can help by revealing another dimension.

The Moon-Node horoscope is a mirror horoscope. This horoscope has to do with subliminal conditions, and lies at the deepest levels of the mind—the region of the collective unconscious. It opens a pathway into this collective unconscious. From the point of view of normal secular psychology we can say that the Moon-Node horoscope indicates the "shadow" personality. We house a shadow, an invisible component of our being, full of motives and wishes, projections, and other contents that are hardly ever available to consciousness and sometimes not at all. What is more, we repress them because they are unusable or even dangerous as far as everyday life is concerned. It is usual and normal to regard this shadow as negative or black, because it is a region lying in the shadow of the light of our consciousness, our Sun on which we rely. Strictly speaking, all of us are night-blind in this region. But as we gradually discern our shadow part, and perceive contrasts that were previously unobserved, then we become complete human beings. We no longer repress certain contents that have a determining influence on us, and we are able to live as whole individuals.

At the time of writing, it is only the depth psychologists who have investigated the properties of the shadow. In this region are to be found all the secret impulses to which we human beings will not admit. Nevertheless, they do influence us; although, generally speaking we are not aware of them as such, since they take the form of reactions and unconscious projections. They come disguised as situations, circumstances and persons into our lives. There seems to be a law at work, which ensures that our repressed secret wishes are turned into magnets for situations, opportunities and people. We experience them as coming from outside, not as belonging to ourselves, and are therefore unable to handle them.

This dimension, which we have just tried to present in purely psychological terms, can be seen somewhat differently. It can be seen, in a religious or esoteric context, as involving predestination of fate. We can call it the deepest layer that influences our lot in life. It is impossible to get to the bottom of it, even with the help of the Moon-Node horoscope. We may think of it as a causal chain, every link of which is out of sight except the final one leading to our present condition. This last link is the state of the unborn, of the resting soul, which does not yet think of being born but is fully formed.

From a Christian standpoint we can say: God has created me, and this is the inner guiding image He employed. It existed before I entered into life. When I came into the world, I was provided with an inherited structure, and as time goes by I am being further shaped by the environment. Each of these contributes to my total character. But the primary layer is already there. In this layer of my being I can see no causalities, and have to accept that I was created as I am.

Then there is the so-called esoteric view, which postulates a causal chain of reincarnation. According to the doctrine of reincarnation, this primary layer, though already in existence, is not a structure bestowed by God or by a higher power, but is something I have made for myself in former lives. Thus I am obliged to bear the consequences of my doings. We shall be looking at this more closely in Part 2.

Anyway, whether a higher power or my past selves are responsible, the outcome is the same: I have to deal with the way I am structured.

How is the Moon-Node Horoscope Calculated?

Our next step deep into the underworld of the unconscious is a scientific one, and has to do with the line of nodes connected with our own Moon-system, which tells us something about our past. Technically, the Moon-Node horoscope is a set of astrological houses specific to the Moon's orbit.

The center of the orbit is the earth; the Moon goes around the Earth in 28 days, and starting from the (ascending and descending) line of nodes we can make 30-degree divisions. From the point of view of Earth, the Moon's orbit is divided into 30-degree sections and incorporated in the horoscope. See figure 8 below.

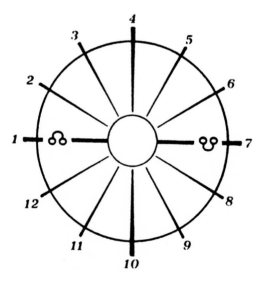

Figure 8. The Moon-Node Houses.

The circle is standardized by using nodal points to mark its beginning and end. In the orbit of the Sun, the first point of Spring is in Aries, and the circle closes in Pisces. In the house system, we take the Ascendant as the beginning: this is the point where the Eastern horizon and the zodiac intersect; that is to say, it is a nodal point. In the Moon-Node horoscope we take the Ascending Node as the beginning, and the nodal line plays a role similar to that of the horizon joining the Ascendant and the Descendant. The Ascending Node is the Ascendant and the Descending Node is the Descendant of the node horoscope.

Now it has to be borne in mind that the Moon's nodal system runs backward. We must follow this movement. It mirrors everything in reverse. The Node house system runs clockwise, counter to the path of the zodiac, and each house has exactly 30 degrees.

The most useful way to erect the Moon-Node horoscope is to have the houses running as normal and the zodiac running in the opposite sense. This is easier to work with. (We employ this method in the horoscope examples in Part 2 of this book—calculated and drawn by the API-Computer Cortex.)

A further point to note is that we enter the buried dimension via the nodal system. The nodal system is our access to this region of the Shadow. The one item borrowed from the house system of the birth chart is the Ascendant, because it represents the climb back into the upper world. The AC of the natal chart becomes the Node in the Moon-Node horoscope, and the AC of the Moon-Node horoscope becomes the Node in the natal chart. We indicate the aspects because aspects to the Node are important, since they represent our links with the upper world. Aspects to the radical Node are indicated, too, as being relevant to our progress. In the Moon-Node horoscope, the Ascendant is an "access road" to our current situation, or a "cellar ladder" that takes us above what is being projected by the past in our Moon-Node horoscope. We must not lose sight of it or we shall be unable to find our way back. Radical aspects to the birthchart Node are left out of account, however, so the aspect picture is not the same as usual.

The Moon-Node Houses and their
Archetypal Definitions

Here, then, are new houses, although we could call them old, seeing they are deeply immersed in the past. The question is, can
these houses of the Node system be judged in the same way as we
judge the ordinary houses? Yes and no. It is still the same house
system: not some new-fangled invention but the age-old result of
observation. Nevertheless it would be rash to assume that the old
definitions can be adopted without more ado. Some people try to
do this, but without success, because modern human beings and
their civilization (in America or Europe say) differ from the
Ancients, even in their standards of measurement. Our definition
of the ordinary houses is culture-dependent, and is a Middle European way of looking at things. Probably it is a North American way
also, and maybe a South American; but certainly not a Japanese,
Chinese, or Filipino way.

To discuss the past as shown by the chart, we have to adopt a
new form of speech that remains valid even when times change,
i.e., is not culture-dependent like our own. Here in the Moon-
Node horoscope we have to find definitions that are archetypal
and, as such, universal, and applicable to every culture and to
every period of history. The task is not easy but, without laying
claim to completeness, we can offer a rough guide to this mode of
thought—which gives more scope for creativity and personal
effort.

These archetypal images confronted us in many people with
whom we studied their Moon-Node horoscopes in the light of
depth psychology. At a given stimulus word, images rose to the surface; buried experiences were resurrected, and suddenly material-
ized in waking consciousness.

Everything was symbolic and expressed itself in two main
forms. In other words, what could be predicated of a given house
with its domiciled planets was twofold: on the one hand, there
were typical figures for that house and, on the other hand, typical
situations for that house. The figures were symbolized by the plan-

ets standing in the house, and the situations were symbolized by the house itself.

Traditionally there are twelve houses, and these cover every possible situation in our lives. It may seem incredible that the whole vast extent of life, which far from being simple is highly complex, could be basically summed up by these twelve houses. But, of course, we are dealing not only with twelve houses, but with twelve signs and ten planets and with all their possible combinations and planetary aspects. We shall now try to formulate the typical figures and the typical situations in the twelve houses that are likely to crop up when we study the Moon-Node horoscope. Since we are dealing with symbols, these archetypical images will also be suitable for working with dreams, especially in connection with the horoscope.

1st Moon-Node House

A character steps out from behind the curtain and says: "Hi, I'm here!" He is the play's hero. His gestures are expansive and he does his best to make a favorable impression. This is the archetypal figure of the 1st house, who can appear in various guises according to the planets occupying that house. The part of our actor is taken by the planet or planets, and the stage setting in which he appears is represented by the astrological house. In the 1st house, this setting is nothing more than the curtain in front of which the actor steps. We can imagine, for example, that Virgo in the 1st house would be equivalent to a curtain of plain hand-woven cloth, while Aquarius would be pure silk, Cancer a jazzy colored fabric, and Leo a thick satin or heavy velour. The setting is decided by the nature of the sign. Now, if we take a look at the 1st house in the Moon-Node horoscope—remembering, of course, that Moon-Node houses run clockwise, so that the Moon-Node 1st house occupies the same position as the radical 12th house—we can analyze it along the above lines. If the sign sets the scene, any planets in the house will represent the player. After the stage entry (so to speak), the audience takes notice of the backdrop and of the appearance and gestures of the player, and listens to what the latter has to say for himself or herself.

Whole histories can rise out of the unconscious in pictorial form (pictorial because often they are beyond description), and this resurfacing of images and experiences occurs as we study the Moon-Node horoscope. To be of any use to us, the experiences must be factual. If nothing happens in a given house, we should leave it and move on to the next. It is better not to linger, otherwise the unconscious will feel compelled to produce something for our benefit, and will come up with a fantasy—and what would be the use of that?

2nd Moon-Node House

In the 2nd house we can picture ourselves as a landowner who possesses the whole surrounding district, and employs everybody else. A big wall encloses the estate to keep out enemies. What does this illustrate? It illustrates how I fence myself in for a peaceful life, and hide my territory and property behind walls, in order to demarcate them and to protect them from the outside world. This picture symbolizes a love of possessions, and possibly greed or covetousness, too; also the tendency to let fly at people who come close enough to filch anything.

The background of our scene is formed by the wall, which cuts off whatever lies on the other side. The wall may not really be depicted, it may be taken for granted; nevertheless, whatever there is to see is on the inside of the wall. Or the stage might have bars at the back; bars which have been bolted on the inside. This is a real possibility; life being played out where there are seemingly no exits and no further input. The suggestion of consolidated gains can be heightened here by the stage props; especially if the actor makes play with what is supposed to belong to him or her—

perhaps as a miser sitting on top of a sack of gold, perhaps as someone with an estate erecting notices that warn: "Trespassers will be prosecuted." Such pictures have the simplicity of fairy-tale scenes and the reader should allow for the fact that, like those, they tend to be overdrawn.

3rd Moon-Node House

Two or more figures are the norm in the 3rd house, because it corresponds to Gemini, the Twins. Often we need to visualize a throng; such as, for example, a troupe of clowns capering in the street, making a hullabaloo, and changing places in a bewildering game. When people hobnob with one another in carnival masks, they are communicating but, at the same time, getting in on the act and saying: "Here I am, I'm one of you, I'm with it!" Usually, in the 3rd house, one does not take oneself too seriously.

On the other hand, the 3rd house can produce the opposite effect: the devoted teacher, who takes himself or herself very seriously indeed. Any schoolteacher who knows everything the pupils need to know ought to be treated with respect, and is not a figure of fun. The clowns are out of place here. If they enter the classroom they must sit down and keep quiet.

So, in the 3rd house, we have two very different individuals occupying the same space. One individual specializes in "horizontal" knowledge, while the other specializes in "vertical" knowledge. The horizontal form of communication and of transmitting knowledge may be observed in exchanges between people meeting on the street or sitting in the square. They know practically all there is to know about one another and swap items of news; and they like having a joke about anyone who seems a little out of the ordinary. The vertical form of communication involves constant learning (as in class) from those who know more than oneself. Knowledge is enlightenment, and light usually shines down on us—so authority is implied here.

The place of instruction is either the street and the market place, where everyone gathers, or the schoolhouse and the lecture room (possibly in a convent or seminary). These are the archetypal elements, always found in the first three signs and the first three houses. They stand for all the rest, which are really only repetitions.

The 1st house also symbolizes the birth of the native, who steps from behind the curtain and says, "Here I am, accept me for myself."

In the 2nd house, the native is already someone, and owns a slice of the world. So, of course, placements in the 2nd house of the Moon-Node horoscope show how we behave or have behaved toward possessions. These are deep-rooted structures, inaccessible to the conscious mind, yet they determine how we handle property in our environment.

In the 3rd house we have the first authentic social relationship and an active mind that is eager to learn.

4th Moon-Node House

The 4th house can be pictured as a motherly soul with her children playing nearby and running up to her, or as a cosy candle-lit room, comfortably furnished and with a warm stove or fireplace. Again, it may remind us of a sunny room where family and friends can meet in safety. This is the basic concept of the 4th house. It is the experience of belonging, of snugness, warmth and being well looked after, of something natural and reassuring.

The mother-figure fits the house perfectly: the house is a mother of a sort, and always gives a sense of security. Alternatively, it can be depicted as a medieval city enclosed by walls, with towers looking down on the clustered roofs; this, too, conveys a feeling of security and is an appropriate picture.

Another figure is that of a mayor and aldermen working for the prosperity and safety of their town. The protective maternal quality is embodied here in an institution. It is men who usually make up this archetypal image but they are protectively equipped with a great golden chain and padded robe, rather like a mother-figure.

5th Moon-Node House

For the 5th house, we can imagine that we are gazing over this medieval city with high walls and roofs until our eyes rest for a moment on the city-gate. A young traveling journeyman is leaving by it, and the world fills him with delight and wonder. This is quite an important figure in the 5th house: "one who travels to know what shivering means" [Grimm], someone who looks very strong and healthy, and is keen to exchange the confines of the city for the open country in order to learn about life. Here, therefore, the countryside is the main symbol. The city stands in the background; as does the farmstead from which a son sets out to serve his apprenticeship and spend his year of travel.

In principle, I am drawn out into the wide world and I go to meet it with open arms. In the 5th house I have to leave home and explore the world, in order to become someone in this world.

Pictures such as the above teach us that we should be responsive to (or at least aware of) the far horizon. But, should Saturn be in the Moon-Node 5th house, we may be deterred by those who would dissuade us from venturing out. "The world is a dangerous place; stay at home!" they cry, and so they may prevent us from gaining the necessary experience. In which case, although we can form some idea of the world we do not really know it.

6th Moon-Node House

A good image of the 6th house is the laborer with bent back who finds life a struggle. Grandiose plans are no use on their own in the 6th house: hard toil is the order of the day. The archetype here is the working man or woman, and the environment is enclosed; it consists of somewhere where work is performed.

Our place of employment is always a limitation. We must work for a living; and, in order to do so effectively, are obliged to concentrate on the job in hand. This automatically restricts our view of the world. It is well known that the analogous sign, Virgo, loses itself in minutiae and often fails to see connections; although it does see quite clearly what needs to be done.

Here, then, we have a small stage in which certain business has to be transacted. It may be occupied by other workers who look on and ask: "What is he doing, how good is he, how does he do his work? Is he conscientious, careful, and full of a sense of duty?" Such things are important in this house.

7th Moon-Node House

A bridal pair makes a good picture of the 7th house, which is the classic house of marriage and exudes a certain air of optimism—just as a wedding does. A great deal depends on what is brought to a marriage, and how far each one is prepared to give what the other wants. In certain planetary positions, problems can arise, e.g., there is a reluctance to enter into a partnership for fear of the consequences. One invariably becomes involved with the wrong partner, or does not get on well with the partner (and may dream of being with someone else). Usually something is wrong somewhere, and we have to go back to the radix to see what planets occupy the 7th house there so that we can compare them with the Moon-Node horoscope. However, a 7th house full of planets can signify that past experience has already made us completely familiar with this area and all its ins and outs. Many have had enough of it and wish to be on their own, especially if there are no planets in the radical 7th house. However, the 7th house has a number of other representative figures: for example, two individuals who do business together. Then there are the trader and the commercial traveler; for the public is always in the background of the 7th house.

8th Moon-Node House

In the 8th house we are again involved with the public, only on a larger scale. We are no longer dealing with a few spectators but with the whole of society. Here we are concerned with a collective, with the human social structure.

Typical figures are the judge, the soldier, the policeman, and the revenue officer. The schoolteacher could be included if a disciplinarian; the essential feature being that of someone ready to lay down the law or take punitive action. This is never taken on the basis of personal opinion but always in the name of society. The mandate is issued by the group, and the judgment can be either negative or positive. It is practically impossible not to feel that one is under pressure; for who likes to be judged? This feeling can be represented by a dark and sinister scene, such as a tribunal. The atmosphere is rather cold and gray, and by no means as cheerful as that of the 7th house. The 7th house is usually sunny, and when something negative occurs it does so suddenly and unexpectedly and it does not completely alter the scene.

In the 8th house, on the other hand, the scene is subdued, dark, and gloomy from the first. Here the 7th house discovers its limitations, just as the 5th house discovers its limitations in the 6th. Active houses are invariably followed by passive houses, and the latter always set limits to the former.

In the 7th house, one enters into partnership with high hopes and, in the 8th house, one is confronted by hard reality, by laws. Here everything has boundaries and one must pay strict attention to them, so as not to make a false move, otherwise there will be unpleasant repercussions.

The 8th house has a wide range of human types at its disposal. The more consciously we live in the 8th house (i.e., the more planets are found there), the more familiar we shall become with these types. Some we meet may be archetypal figures. The judge, for example, is an archetypal figure. However, if Mars or Venus is posited in the 8th house, animal forms may rise from buried layers of the unconscious. Dark, demonic figures can also appear, representing an even deeper scrutiny of our doings—one which cannot be argued away. Here the primitive corporeal manifestation is usually involved. Demons show themselves when the world of the body or of the psyche is out of sorts. When reserves are low, disorders occur, and our surroundings look bleak. As a matter of fact, water plays a role here; "lake-monsters" can surface, together with various legendary scenes from the Underworld. Often there emerge, from some abyss, forces that affect our physical state. And the nature of the sign has a lot to do with the extent to which the instinctual area is involved.

9th Moon-Node House

The 9th is another of the active houses, and it gives us scope to be more enterprising. In the 9th house, we again find someone out to conquer the world; interestingly enough, rapid movement often plays a part in this. The central figure is mobile and can, for example, be a knight riding through the land, this being one of the archetypal forms of the 9th house. In the background everything may look dark, but the quarter toward which the horseman is galloping is bright. Frequently the countryside is open, and the steed can be given its head. Of course, the scene can be updated to feature a stagecoach, a locomotive, or even a plane—all rushing past.

High points here are the mobility and the distant goal. In this imagery, we invariably encounter open countryside and the light toward which one travels. The latter tells of hope, and hope decidedly belongs to the 9th house; but it also signifies exploration, an attempt to reach beyond the seen. The blue horizon always beckons where the landscape melts away, for the 9th house has to do with the search for ultimate truth. The main character can be a traveling journeyman going far, or the familiar Fool of the Tarot. The Fool steps away toward the distance, led by something unknown. The far-away light stands for the enlightenment for which we hope when seeking supreme truth, knowledge, and wisdom.

10th Moon-Node House

For most of us, height somehow plays a part in the 10th house. We find ourselves somewhere high, or climb a mountain. For people who live in a flat land, the high spot is a tall building or a tower, representing an upward movement or a vantage point with a wide view. If one is not already there, then one is well on the way to this elevated position. The symbolic figure is very variable, and can be young or old; the difference depends on the planetary placement.

The height to be scaled takes different forms according to the region in which the native is born and bred; as will already have been gathered. Frequently in the 11th house, and occasionally here in the 10th, the symbolism involves personages such as kings, senators, cardinals, deities, and saints. We find it in horoscopes of people who live very instinctively: this 10th-house tendency is projected largely on the outside world, and the natives long to meet some such elevated person who would be willing to help them.

Often the native appears on stage, perhaps as a speaker or an actor, and receives applause, yet always fears lack of approval.

11th Moon-Node House

Here we almost invariably have a limited group of between five and (at most) twenty persons; usually people commanding respect or seeming to be important—more often in spiritual or intellectual matters than in mundane ones. They could be earls, princesses, pharaohs, or Knights Templar. Lecturers or professors often enter the picture, but even more often priests, or figures from myths or sagas. Thus symbolic images of two types are possible.

In the first version, the native sees himself or herself as one of these elevated beings or belongs to a group of them; the scenery is then mainly open, and there are temple-like buildings or a sun-lit landmark (usually set on a hill). In the second version, the native sees himself or herself as small and insignificant in comparison with such sublime figures. Occasionally, angels appear too, descending from or ascending to heaven, or the individual floats in ethereal regions—like a dreamer—maybe wafted by supporting wings.

12th Moon-Node House

Here we have many and varied motifs; the simplest being that of standing on the edge of an abyss, afraid of falling into it and then actually doing so. Mostly this lies in the instinctive region. The fear is frequently of a bottomless pit which has a devouring quality. Our surroundings are dark; often, all that can be seen is the black hole, the rest is a blur; the infinite universe is shut out and we are hemmed in by fog.

As is well known, the 12th house has to do with disintegration or transcendence, so there are two possibilities: living in fear of plunging into the abyss is one of them, the other is the freedom to soar (unaided) into space. These are the two extremes, but between them there are variations, such as trembling in the balance, being depressed, being pushed into a corner, etc. Also, the lighting symbolism is important and should be noted. It can be dark grayish-blue like that of an electric storm, or blindingly bright. The color violet sometimes plays a part, and angelic beings can hover near; but so can demonic figures and batlike or weird creatures, which are unnerving and simply serve to increase the fear and uncertainty. Space assumes great importance, whether it takes the form of shafts descending to unfathomable depths or the form of infinite cosmic space.

The Moon-Node Horoscope as an Inner Capacity

When looked at from another point of view, the Moon-Node horoscope represents a compilation from one's past; not, as might easily be supposed, any particular former life. The way to look at it is that we have lived different lives, and have now returned to Earth in order to make further progress. The lives now gone exhibited a basic theme, because there are one or two leading themes that occupy us through life, and there are subsidiary themes which are not so important. It is also entirely possible, and indeed quite probable, that only one theme will be present during our life.

By making strenuous efforts to overcome certain vital problems, we develop strong abilities. These abilities have a permanent value. They remain with us as abstract powers, which carry over into the next incarnation. They are not external concrete entities. For example, if I have learned in one of my lives to be a joiner and have been very proficient, have worked well, and have become renowned for my skill in handling the tools of my trade, this does not mean that I shall return to earth next time as a master joiner able to carry on where I left off. No, the formal details of the craft will be lost to me. What remains is the love of wood as a material and of tools of a specific type, and a feeling for the structural principles of furniture-making—these are what I take with me in all subsequent lives; they are permanent qualities or talents, denoted somewhere in the horoscope. If I have done anything well in one or more lives, a strong imprint of my activity remains, and often appears in the chart as a talent triangle. Its origin has absolutely no bearing on my further development. What matters is that it is now at my disposal as an acquired quality. Of course, in each life I have to relearn how to exploit it.

The Moon-Node horoscope does not show when or where I learned something, but does show the theme on which I have concentrated intensely (for a longer or shorter period) in order to acquire a given quality. This is a potential, even if it is inactive in my present life. Once it was in play, now perhaps it is in the waiting mode at a Low Point, and later on it may again take part in my development. The Low Point positions of planets indicate inner potentials that can be harnessed at some time.

Numerous studies are currently being made on people professing to have very circumstantial memories of former lives. However, it is not essential to my development that I should know all the ins and outs; the essential thing is what the past has taught me.

Those interested in reincarnation may try to gain some knowledge of their former lives by consulting the Moon-Node horoscope. The danger of that is getting lost in the past and losing touch with the present. Everything depends on recognizing our structural patterns, so that we can then access our deep-lying motivations. Many such structures are present in the Moon-Node horoscope, and their effect is to make us prisoners of destiny. They are suppressing and bottling up inside us energies which are liable to escape from the bottle after a while and to materialize outside us like a temperamental genie. Our fate appears to be in the hands of something irrational, and there is nothing we can do.

Chapter 6

The Three Horoscopes

The Radix or Natal Horoscope • The House Horoscope • The Moon-Node Horoscope • Comparison of the Radix and the Moon-Node Horoscope • Evolution in the Three Horoscopes •

Three Horoscopes

Three horoscopes can be erected for every nativity, and they represent different facets of human consciousness, knowledge, and experience. Their psychological differences will be explained at the end of the book by means of two illustrative examples.

The Radix or Natal Horoscope

The usual horoscope is called the radix or natal horoscope, and is based on measurement applied to the zodiac. It is this horoscope that informs us about our state of consciousness in everyday life, as represented by the Sun. The Sun, in its annual journey, maps our the zodiac for us; so we do well to look at things from the solar point of view and to make it fundamental to our thinking. When we realize that the radix is the chart of everyday consciousness, we can see that it gives us a thoroughly rational approach to the native. Its domain is the same as the one that modern psychology seeks to explore; but astrology, through the study of the horoscope, is able to bring us much closer to a complete and comprehensive understanding of the individual.

The House Horoscope

Our second horoscope is the house horoscope, and commences at the Ascendant. Its houses are all 30 degrees wide, because they are equally important in subjective experience. The house horoscope is like the cross-wires of a telescopic sight through which we view the universe, the starry world, and of course the zodiac. The zodiac is seen objectively and no longer looks like a circle but like an ellipse, and its signs vary in size.

This second horoscope has its own aspect configuration: the angles of the aspects change when the house system is used to measure them. Essentially, the houses represent the environment, which consists of concrete, tangible situations; being made up, on the one hand, of nature, civilization, and forms of society, and, on the other hand, of the people living in them. These people and things, individually or collectively, have a powerful influence on us, because they are all part of the web of life. They make a deep impression on our conscious minds and we are forced to adapt to them, more or less. Their effects on us are symbolized by the house aspects.

We can see the house horoscope as a determining factor in the here and now (it is therefore one-dimensional in time), and also as an incentive to further development. By highlighting the influence of our surroundings, it indicates the forces of change that are affecting us. It does not show the end-product, but simply these forces of change. Thus we find ourselves not in a deterministic structure, where we know how things will fall out, but in a situation where we have a considerable say as to how far we will change under the forces that are working on us. We can resist them or cooperate with them. However, even while cooperating, we may perhaps change in ways that are neither compulsory nor necessarily shown in the chart. This is where free will enters the picture.

In a spiritual sense there can be no clear and unambiguous fate for human beings. All that we have are conditionalities that restrict our freedom of movement, some of which we bring with us and into some of which we are born. But we are always left with some scope for using our will and judgment. Not only can we help to determine our rate of development, but in principle we can produce new qualities that are not even indirectly indicated. Recognition that we have this freedom is the only healthy approach to astrology. Any other attitude always returns us to fatalism, to a belief in strictly predetermined structures that compel us to function in such and such a way. The environment is a tool of destiny that challenges us to cope with constraints and use them to promote our personal growth. The house horoscope shows how the environment "provokes" us to develop.

The Moon-Node Horoscope

The third horoscope is the Moon-Node horoscope.[1] The Ascendant of the Node horoscope is the Moon's Node in the natal chart. Using that as a starting point, we count backward 30 degrees in a clockwise direction and reach the cusp of the 2nd house, and so on. Obviously, the various planets of the radix are likely to be found in quite different houses here. And, in this way, subliminal motivations come to light which, although their effects have been plain enough, have not previously been recognized as belonging to ourselves.

The Moon-Node horoscope contains the familiar twelve houses, the areas embodying twelve different motivations (any of which can be diversified if several planets occupy a house). Our basic desires cover twelve domains, and it is important to try to understand them.

Although it is not permissible to do so in the two horoscopes already described, in the Moon-Node horoscope we may study

---

[1]The three-chart printout is available from API(UK) Chart Data Service, or can be generated by software programs generating Huber-style charts. See page x.

each house in complete isolation. We can define each position just as it stands, because in our lives there are individual requirements in the areas specified. The whole world lies before the emotional "I" represented by the Moon, and this emotional part of us has the ability to see this whole world as a unit; but the view is wholly subjective, it is certainly not logical. The Moon, the emotions, and the mainspring of the unconscious, do not employ logic. They follow an absolute dictate: "I am and I will."

The Moon-Node horoscope, which may also be called the mirror horoscope, is somewhat obscure to the conscious mind; it is not very graphic, and it shows us things reversed as in a mirror. Therefore we are inclined to refuse and repress its contents. They lie very deep in the unconscious, yet they are reflected in the Moon-Node horoscope, and they become the shadow. Frequently we are troubled and thrown into confusion by them. On the other hand, there are many occasions when we experience one of them rising up inside us, and promptly interpret it the wrong way round, e.g., in a dream. Admittedly, when we are dreaming, the reversal in space is less noticeable, but the events are usually out of sequence. However, because our rational mind expects events to be in sequence, it seldom doubts their order of occurrence in dreams. But we should be making a big mistake to assume that dream sequences can be transferred to everyday life without more ado. Often we can check this, when we dream of real things that we have already experienced or will experience later in life. It is more confusing when time undergoes a mirror-effect than when objects are reflected the "wrong way round" in space. We find it easier to allow for the latter reversal. Precognitive dreams are more often experienced by people with parapsychological faculties. Now precognition is a mirror effect in time; therefore periods of time are often misjudged because they are out of sequence in a vision, or because the length of time involved is not what it seems to be. One assumes, perhaps, that everything will come about in a few days, whereas in reality several years are involved.

Many a psychic content that has made its presence felt in our lives has inverse proportions in the mirror sphere of the Moon-

Node horoscope or in the shadow personality; and these indicate motivations that have been repressed, because we have been unable to integrate them properly—and so they appear to us to be the wrong way round. This then is the mechanism with which we are confronted in the Moon-Node horoscope, and it is something we shall need to look at in further detail.

In the radix, the Ascendant represents the place of the "I," where we see ourselves. And the Descendant is the place where we see the "You." And in these two places we inscribe "I" and "You," or, in other words, express what we think about our own ego and about our opposite number. These opinions induce us to behave in a certain way when we meet the other person. And our attitude is a rational one, i.e., it is consciously formulated. It may be differentiated to a greater or lesser extent but, in any case, it is accessible to the conscious mind. Even if we are not much interested in self-portrayal, we do have a self-image; and the self-image determines our behavior toward our contacts. Our blueprint of the "You" helps us to be selective in our encounters.

In the Moon-Node horoscope the "You" changes place with the "I," which suggests that even in the radix the house system could be seen reversed. A pattern of values emerges from the right-left system: the right has a specific value, and the left has a specific value. Similar patterns arise in all cultures.

As is well known, some languages are written from right to left, while others are written from left to right. There seems to be a mirror phenomenon here. The values we have assigned still hold good, but what happens is that if someone always writes from left to right, then a vast number of left-to-right movements will be carried out during life. This is typically Western and individualistic, but cannot be taken as the only proper way.

The individual who writes from right to left, moves (as we would say) from the other person to the self; or, if passive toward life and humanity, may let the "You" walk all over him or her. This reverses reality. The "I" is no longer so tremendously important.

Curiously enough, it is almost always an "I"-"You" relationship that finds expression in the Moon-Node horoscope. If we want to understand it, we can take as a yardstick our attitude to the environment, the give and take between the "I" and the "You," and the motivations involved. For we cannot help being motivated, whether we are approaching the "You" or are deciding to welcome or rebuff the "You" approaching us.

Comparison of the Radix and Moon-Node Horoscope

We have motivations that are conscious and known, and we have others (so it would seem) that are unknown. The latter can determine our behavior to an equal, or even to a greater, extent. Therefore it is good to know what motivations we really have. To interpret planetary placements in the Moon-Node horoscope, we need bear in mind the planetary placements by sign in the radix, for these forces are still present and active in the Moon-Node horoscope. They are our primary resource. The Moon-Node horoscope reveals the motivations we apply to these forces in the radix. We must set the one over against the other, so that the "I" and the "You" overlap. Everything is dual in this formation, and everything can be seen in reverse—as in a mirror.

Therefore we must correctly identify the placement of each planet in the natal chart in its sign and house, and above all, try to determine how it operates and how it is motivated by the conscious mind.

The radix, then, has to be compared with the Moon-Node horoscope. If two placements in the two systems coincide, that is to say if, for example, there is a planet in the same house in both, then no change is indicated, and we have a deep awareness of our motivation. More will be said about this in Part 2. Here it may be mentioned that we do need a point of reference to avoid losing our way in irrational speculation. And, in fact, we have to be guided by how we are affected. Values or norms can have no force here. If we do attempt to make a comparison of motivations according to some predetermined value, we find that everything reverses itself and throws us into confusion. A good example of what is meant is the astronaut who finds during a space flight that the distinction between up and down has disappeared. The only reference he has is his own body: where his head happens to be is up, and where his feet are is down.

Evolution in the Three Horoscopes

The three horoscopes express a dynamic stretch of time—a mechanism of development. An individual is intended to develop like the plant from the seed, which grows and flowers, and then, after it has produced fruit, dies, bequeathing a kernel of renewal inside this fruit.

Plants evolve, too—along with animals and human beings. And, of course, human beings undergo biological development; but what is important is that they experience a development of the conscious mind. In essence, our awareness of the world and, above all, of ourselves in the world, changes and undergoes a process of evolution. Many individuals pass through this unconsciously, being ruled by fate. Others try to accelerate their development and steer it in a certain direction.

Evolution of this sort is exhibited in the above mentioned three horoscopes. The Moon-Node horoscope symbolizes the past, the radix the present, and the house horoscope the impetus toward future development given by the environment. The Moon-Node horoscope enshrines those primary conditions which, having been created by ourselves, supply certain hopes for our lives that we would like to see fulfilled.

Each hidden desire, as indicated by the Moon-Node horoscope, leaves behind in us, in the course of time, a powerful urge with corresponding compulsive behavior and attendant guilt feelings, and can become a driving force in life. We have little idea of the number of compulsive mechanisms and guilt feelings with which we function. The Moon-Node horoscope shows past

achievements, in which specific aspirations slumber yet are opera-
tive in the present. To put it in a nutshell: what we expect is contained in the Moon-Node horoscope; what the world expects of us
is visible in the House Horoscope.

The House Horoscope is rather like a toolmaker. The conception, and the view of my person, held by the world, are projections; and the world's educational measures would make an imple-
ment out of me. But I, too, have an influence on the product, to
the extent that I recognize my own expectations arising out of the
past and also recognize my current options.

Thus it depends on my degree of awareness, whether I can
resist the influence of others or succumb to it. If the conditions
are right, I may even retard or stop what they are doing. So I can
have some say in the working of the formative forces that are act-
ing on me. The House Horoscope is no cut-and-dried model of
the future, but is a model of the forces that are tending to mold
me for the future. As it happens, they are the very forces needed
for my further development. The horoscope reveals the environment to which, so far, I have partially been subject. Now the more
I know about the different layers of my being, the more decision-
making I can take into my own hands.

Chapter 7

The Moon's Node
and the Age Point

The Age Point • Crossing Point and Opposition • Fundamental
Themes of the Life • Age-Point Crossing Points on the House Axes
• Encounter Axis 1/7 • Possession Axis 2/8 • Thought Axis 3/9 •
Individuality Axis 4/10 • Relationship Axis 5/11 • Existence Axis
6/12 • Encounter Axis and the Moon-Node Line •

The Age Point

The Moon-Node horoscope has an Age Point of its own. That is to say, it contains a time element with much the same mechanism as the ordinary Age Point. In the natal chart, the houses are each transited over a six-year period, but as their sizes differ, their step-by-step divisions are larger or smaller, too. In the Moon-Node horoscope, the divisions are equal and can be read from the zodiac at the rate of five degrees per year. The Moon-Node Age Point runs backward against the cosmic motion, i.e., it moves clockwise (see figure 9 on page 114). If we take a look at the radical Age Point and at its Moon-Node counterpart, we shall see how their relationship works.

The radical Age Point shows how we engage in activities with a great show of reason, so that intelligible psychological processes seem to underlie our experiences and everything we do. But the Moon-Node horoscope shows what our subliminal self really wants to do, and what we wish to achieve—although we may not be prepared to admit it. This gives us a much more profound understanding of why we take such pains to have every detail rationally nailed down.

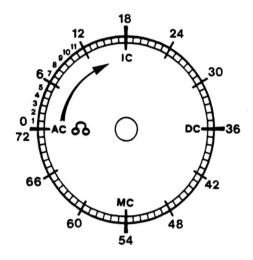

Figure 9. The MN dial.

Crossing Point and Opposition

Meeting Point of the Moon-Node Age Point and the Radical Age Point

The radical Age Point, which follows the cosmic rotation, and the Moon-Node Age Point, which moves in the opposite direction, meet twice during the 72 years taken by each of them to make a complete circuit of the horoscope; and 36 years after their second encounter, they will meet for a third time if the native lives well beyond the age of 72. Their first encounter will occur during the first 36 years of life at a time depending on the position of the Moon's Node, and their second encounter will occur 36 years later. When, for example, the first encounter takes place at age 14 (in the 3rd house), a third encounter is indicated (in the 3rd house again) at age 86. Another vital landmark is the opposition of the two Age Points. This also happens every 36 years.

The conjunctions and oppositions of the two Age Points can be very significant, because they are meeting points on the temporal plane. Now the nodal line (the line joining the Ascending and the Descending Nodes) marks the transition from the lower to the upper horoscope, from the everyday personality to the shadow (which is derived from the past and is represented by the Moon-Node horoscope). This is the spatial dividing line. But there is also a temporal dividing line between the two "vital" areas—the line joining the places at which the two Age Points meet (C1 and C2). See figure 10 below.

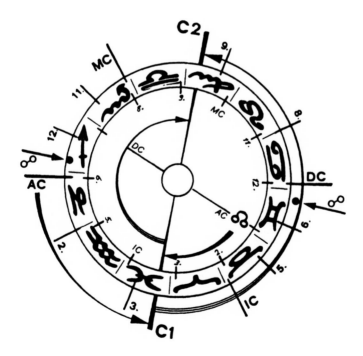

Figure 10. Crossing points, C1 C2.

A note on technique: the two Age Points, the radical Age Point and the Moon-Node Age Point, are taken at their beginning. As we know, they are approaching one another. Their respective annual movements are entered in the chart until they meet. Square to their meeting place is their opposition. This is how the moment of crossing is found.

Strictly speaking, we are not dealing with points in time, so exactness is not required. There can be a spread of up to two years on either side. And an important consideration is whether or not this region of the horoscope is occupied. If, for example, a planet, the beginning or end of a sign, a house cusp, or a Low Point, is near this meeting point or near the point of opposition, the orb can be fairly wide.

For instance, it is possible that specific events that are essential to the experience of personal development do not fall on the exact meeting point, but fall on a meeting point close by where there is a planet, the first or last degree of a sign, a house cusp, etc. So here are four clear-cut occasions in life when we need to take a long hard look at our attitudes and motivation. And as very few of us are prepared to do this on our own initiative, we find that fate does it for us, which can lead to traumatic experiences. In fact, what we are dealing with here is very deep motivation—not in regard to a specific situation, predilection, or ability, but in regard to the "I" itself. In other words the challenge is: how are we conducting ourselves, why are we behaving in one way and not in some other way, and do our current activities promote our development—indeed, what is the meaning of our lives?

This is the most fundamental set of questions fate can ask, and it does pull us up; not abruptly perhaps, but with sufficient braking power for us to realize that there has to be some readjustment. As we stop in this "resting place," so to speak, there is an opportunity to see where we are on the great highway of life. Some life-changing events are like traffic accidents, but things need not happen so suddenly if we start taking stock of our lives in good time. People who put these fundamental questions to themselves, without waiting for fate to do so, will in principle avert various events that might otherwise occur. Something intervenes only when we live aimlessly, chasing phantoms that are altogether external and worldly.

Apparently, what these significant events do is to compel us, somehow or other, to pay attention to the fact that we are not on Earth by chance, free to live just as we like, but are meant to think about why we are here and what we have to learn. Obviously, the matter is one of cause and effect.

Fundamental Themes of the Life
Age-Point Crossing Points in the House Axes

The fundamental problems raised by the Age-Point meeting points in the horoscope are capable of exact formulation if we take into consideration the house axis in which the meeting points occur. We term this the "crossing axis."

There are six fundamental problems that are always posed very urgently by fate at these points. They arise internally, or show themselves in the form of external pressures, or manifest as a combination of the two. We live with a recurring motif. It is better to keep it constantly in view, but at least four times in our lives we are compelled to come to grips with this basic motivation.

So what are these six fundamental themes? They are the qualities of the axes. The orientation of the meeting-point line and of the line of opposition between the two Age Points coincides with some house axis or other, and so reveals what problem is enshrined in the "encounter axis." Although not determinative, a role is played here not only by the houses but also by the signs. The leading role belongs to the houses and their axes; the signs, on the other hand, make up a supporting cast and reveal something about our propensities. The houses and the axes show the present reality. They indicate the theme that is constantly pressing for decisions in this life.

The sign placement gives the quality that, stemming from the past, determines or influences our current attitude.

Since both the meeting point of the two Age Points and their opposition are released in a cross and interpreted as a "whole," the reader is recommended to see what is said about the polarity of the axes in our book, *The Astrological Houses.* The orientation of the axial themes is shown in figure 11 on page 119.

Encounter Axis 1/7

The "I" meets the "You." It is very important for me to know how to meet my world, and this involves two things: I must know who I am, and I must have a good idea of the "You" I am meeting or wish to meet (and know what I want of the "You"). There are always two things to consider in every axis. There has to be a clarification of the realities of contact with my world, especially with those I encounter; and this clarification will help me to meet the individuals who are right for me and share my aspirations. Otherwise my best endeavors will come to nothing. However, when I am aware of what I want and make a sincere effort to achieve it, the right people will cross my path almost automatically.

By clearly formulating the 1/7 axis (the axis concerned with who I am and what I wish to accomplish), I inevitably choose my mode of action and pave the way for success. The motivation imparted by this axis is very important for anyone who wants to be a success—not just a superficial success, but a genuine success in something central to the life that satisfies a creative urge and can benefit others. The 1/7 axis is thus a creative axis, through which we can make an original and lasting contribution to our environment.

Possession Axis 2/8

Our own possessions come in the 2nd house; the possessions of others in the 8th house. Here we have something "substantial," in the form of material wealth, spiritual wealth, or valuable talents and abilities. But the question arises: How can I make an invest-

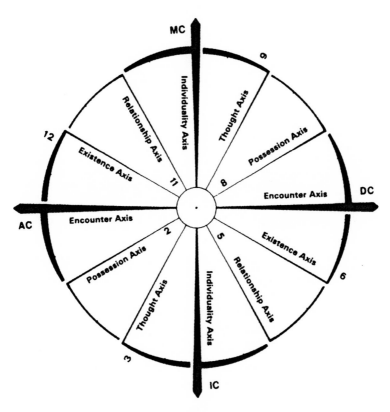

Figure 11. The axis cross in the house system.

ment in the whole of what I have, and how can I receive something from the whole in return? What do I want to achieve, and what is it that brings me satisfaction?

The question of where to draw the line also arises here: How wide should I set my limits, and how wide do I want to set them? Is it right for me—generally speaking—to make demarcations? Where does egoism start, where do I offend others by restricting them too much? This is where one needs to learn the art of drawing the line in the right place. The delicate balance between give and take has to be understood and cultivated. What is more, I need to learn the difference between "yours" and "mine," and to know exactly what I have to give and what I am entitled to receive.

These first two axes are concerned in the widest sense with the old problem of being and having. The first axis has to do with being and the second has to do with having, and both are connected with our status in the world. The world measures us by these two yardsticks.

Thought Axis 3/9

In the third axis the question is: What do we know? How efficiently, how independently, how logically, do we think? The thought axis, too, has two poles. Underneath, in the 3rd house, is the thinking learned from the group in which one grows up and feels at home. It is the thinking that gives one access to one's milieu and social culture, and it is the key to membership of the community.

In the 9th house, a philosophy of life is created by means of logical thought applied to what has been personally observed. The process starts in the 3rd house with hearing the views of others, and ends in the 9th house with the elaboration of a clear-cut set of ideas of one's own. This is the thrust of the 3/9 axis. In this axis, it is not enough to know much; it is important to be able to do something with one's knowledge. Thus if we have the nodal line of intersection, or opposition, on this axis, there can be difficulties, even if these are due simply to the fact that life passes us by, and we lose ground because greater demands are placed on our intelligence than we are able to meet. Then the emphasis is more on the 3rd house.

Another possibility is that we are continually confronted with questions we cannot answer, so that we have to learn to live with these open questions and to resist being influenced by the strong opinions of wiseacres. For the time being, we have to suffer our inability to answer these questions which, for the most part, are about some big connection, about the meaning of something important, or about the meaning of life in general—and can be very tormenting.

The collective will probably be ready with a variety of answers, in the form of philosophies, political theories, religious dogmas, and so on. These answers can be accepted up to a point; but whoever has the 3/9 crossing axis is not likely to be satisfied with them. Such a person has to find his or her own answers, and if they cannot be found today they have to be waited for, even if they are a long time in coming.

The realization: I cannot think of it just now, it is not clear to me, I am unable to answer this question, is in itself a genuine, positive stage of growth. There may be no final answers, but at least there is a willingness to leave certain questions open without resorting to specious reasoning or looking for quick answers. Because knowledge is not enough in this axis; the need is for wisdom in the ultimate and deepest sense.

Individuality Axis 4/10

The 4th house finds us as part of the collective into which we were born, or which we elected to join later in life. This is a group of persons with the same lifestyle as ourselves. No great spiritual harmony is required for people to be able to live together, but a shared lifestyle is essential.

We are given a task by the individuality axis; which, as its name suggests, traces the development of the human being, out of the collective, toward individual status in the 10th house. It implies the courage to detach oneself from others; to say, "This is what I am like and this is where I differ from you." Our own originality has to crystallize out here, and that is something that calls for the courage of our convictions. Thus the 4/10 axis is similar to the 3/9 axis, which also requires courage, in that case the courage to stick to our own, possibly unorthodox, ideas.

In the 10th house, I cannot stand out as an individual unless I am prepared to distance myself from others to some extent. I must be able to go it alone. In the 4/10 axis, the big question is whether I will opt for this quality of individuality and for growth, or will decide against these things and thus remain low-profile and conformist. Making an individual effort in the 10th house may well be a crucial step from which I shrink; yet, if I hold back, life itself can intervene to throw me on my own resources for a while.

Relationship Axis 5/11

Encounter axis and relationship axis are closely similar concepts. Encounter is active, a dynamic process. Relationship is a state; and its axis could also be called the axis of love or friendship or of ethics and morals, except that this easily leads to misunderstandings. In the 11th house one has ethics, in the 5th one observes a moral code. The moral code usually comes from the society in which one lives—it is determined by the social situation and by those with whom one comes in contact. When, for example, I meet a potential sexual partner whom I find strongly attractive but who has a moral code that makes me ineligible, I reach an impasse. My own morals are not the only consideration here; the other person's morals are important, too. The moral code involves our "gut-reactions" whereas ethics are lodged in the head, and important differences spring from this fact at times.

It is interesting that we usually want to have our moral code approved by society, but our ethics need only be approved by ourselves; because the moral 5th house lies in the unconscious, instinctive sector of the chart, on the righthand side or "You" side (which relates to the environment), whereas the ethical 11th house lies in the upper, conscious half of the chart, on the lefthand side, or "I" side.

If someone says of me that I am a moral, irreproachable person, then the 5th-house part of me is gratified, because I need this reassurance. But if, from the heights of my 11th-house ethics, I can look down on others, I feel good in another way. Now this polarity of the relationship axis raises the question of whether the important thing is to feel big and noble, or to express goodness in human relationships and also to make a contribution to society. In other words, is the relationship a living one or is it a mere formality used to impress others or even myself? The touchstone here is the spirit and not the form. And yet, form is particularly accentuated. None are so readily offended as those who have problems in this axis. If the formalities are not preserved, they don't know "what the world is coming to." Nevertheless, we have to break free from forms here and look for genuine living relationships.

Existence Axis 6/12

In the existence axis, we have to do with being or not-being in a this-worldly and an other-worldly sense. The question of existence is asked twice: once in the 6th house and once in the 12th. The 6th, which is deeply involved in the environment and is completely dependent on the world, prompts me to ask: "Am I or am I not going to survive? Have I enough to eat, and can I sleep with a roof over my head?" The 12th house, which stands aloof from the world, is that inner space in which questions concerning existence *per se* are asked, such as: "Do I have a right to live, and is my life useful?"

When the meeting points lie here, these questions become very pointed and, usually, the person's life is put to the test. This can happen through various events or inner experiences, and the life can even be totally negated. For example, one can get into a situation in which it seems impossible to survive. This need not be a case of physical danger, it can be a psychological state in which one is at the end of one's tether; but the test can take a more positive form where one is routinely answerable to others.

It is necessary here to arrive at a state of inner composure in the sense of: I am, therefore it is meaningful that there is such a person as me. This is the final answer, however we may choose to word it. I should embark on life without hang-ups, because life is right in itself and is to be lived on that basis. As long as I avoid this conclusion, I face the risk that life will make me feel that I do not have a right to exist. These are fundamental philosophical questions, like those of the 3/9 axis.

In the second set of three axes, there is a repetition of the first set of three only on a different plane. As already stated, basic motivations of life are formulated in the axes, and these motivations have to be elucidated and ultimately affirmed.

The Crossing Axis and the Moon-Node Line

The crossing axis must not be confused with the Moon-Node line. In the Moon-Node line, the way forward and backward can be discerned, and in the crossing axis a basic theme of life is given.

The Moon's Node, itself, poses no questions, but gives guidance. On the other hand, the axis joining the Age Point meeting points (and that joining the opposition of the two Age Points) keeps repeating the same question at these points. It is no good looking to the Ascending Node for the answer; what that does is give me the means of orienting myself. As just stated, the question has to be faced much more often than one, two, three, or four times. Situations will frequently recur in which I must reason out, assimilate, and persevere, in order to discover if possible a bigger and more profound answer, and it is sensible to use the Moon-Node as a permanent vantage point for this purpose.

The Ascending Node, itself, as we have it in the radix, is the essence of practicality, and shows us the right way to go every time or, if not, at least it indicates the next step. The crossing axis is a large-scale theme of the order of magnitude of a whole life.

Part 2

THE MOON'S NODES AND ESOTERICISM

by
Louise Huber

Chapter 1

Esoteric
Connections

Introduction • What is Meant by Esotericism • The Etheric
Plane and the Moon-Node Horoscope • The Four Subtle
Bodies of the Human Being • Esoteric Definition of the Moon's
Node • Immortality • The Law of Evolution • The Doctrine of
Reincarnation • Reincarnation Therapy • Always Another
Chance • Integration • Release from Guilt • Historical
Awareness • Karma and Dharma • The Shadow • Mirror
Spheres • Reversal • Beyond Good and Evil • The Theory of
Relativity • Synthesis and Understanding • Integration
of the Shadow • Psychological Methods •

Introduction

Many people believe that esotericism is all about parapsychological phenomena, or occult practices such as spiritism, clairvoyance, hypnotism, etc. Often they are unaware that esotericism is, properly speaking, a spiritual path or way of initiation, which in the advanced civilizations of antiquity was a closely guarded secret of the mystery schools. Toward the end of the last century (in 1875), Helena Petrovna Blavatsky, in her book *The Secret Doctrine*,[1] took this knowledge from where it had been preserved by small circles of occultists and made it public. *The Secret Doctrine* became the key book for many esoteric movements. Alice A. Bailey, Rudolf Steiner, Max Heindel, and many

---

[1]H. P. Blavatsky, *The Secret Doctrine* (London: Theosophical Publishing House, 1893). Many modern editions of this book are available.

others, were students of Blavatsky, and they spread her teachings throughout the world in various ways.

Nowadays, more people than ever before take an interest in esoteric matters. As recently as 1973, it was difficult in our astrology courses to say anything about karma and rebirth, let alone to touch on the comprehensive work of Alice Bailey which was our esoteric background. During six active years at the Arkanschule in Geneva and at the Institut für Psychosynthese with Dr. Roberto Assagioli, we were able to study and put into practice the writings of Alice Bailey. Since then we have tried to integrate this knowledge into our astrological system and to facilitate its understanding. The astrological mode of thought has greatly helped here. Since there is an esoteric dimension in the Moon-Node horoscope, we need to know how to handle this. Therefore, in what follows, we shall give a brief account of the esoteric side of the Moon-Node horoscope before considering special astrological methods of interpretation.

What is Meant by Esotericism

Reference to a dictionary reveals that the word "esoteric" is derived from the Greek *esoteros*, which simply means "interior" or "hidden." Therefore "esoteric" is a term for what lies behind external appearance, for those invisible energies that produce the various visible phenomena, bodies, or actions. It relates to the rarefied world of energies and forces, to the essence, self, or soul concealed in the outer form, whether that of a human, a planet, or of some other entity. Such energies can organize an atom, a plant, an animal, or a person. In every case the esoteric factor is the qualitative, vital principle from which the organism draws its life-force.

We see then that esotericism concerns itself with this hidden vital principle, which penetrates and maintains all forms, from the smallest atom through those gigantic aggregates we call planets or solar systems. Therefore it is most important to realize that each of us is no more than a miniscule part of an immeasurable and all-embracing whole, that the energies that drive not only us—but also the totality of existence—are the energies of that one Life "in whom we live and move and have our being." To understand this, we need to know that esotericism teaches that any independence or separation from the whole is only an illusion. From the standpoint of the unity of life, everything that exists comes from a single source. Therefore the study of esotericism is also the search for this primal source; it entails setting out on the "path back to the Father's House" or, as esoteric literature calls it, "the path of initiation." Esoteric astrology is a part of this; because the necessary stages, processes of transformation, and expansions of consciousness, can be identified with the help of the three spiritual planets and the three horoscopes (the Moon-Node, natal, and house horoscopes).

The Etheric World and the Moon-Node Horoscope

The life principle that vitalizes all forms is known as ether in esoteric literature, and *prana* in Indian philosophy. Ether pervades all planes, manipulates their shapes and colors, and in this way continually gives expression to new life-forms. It is present on all seven cosmic planes. The esotericist knows that behind the world of appearances, an etheric, or spiritual, world lies hidden, and that this is the real animating and driving force in each living body. Ether, or the Light of Space, is the channel and field of operations of energies flowing from many sources. The etheric bodies of the whole universe, our planet, and of each individual human being, resemble a golden net consisting of streams of energy. It is in constant motion, and is an eternal medium for the exchange and transmission of energies and information.

The etheric world is the "mysterium magicum," out of which all that exists is born and to which all that exists returns. In other words, ether is the light, *Fohat*, or universal soul, which serves as the matrix of the universe and, in its manifestation on the astral plane, is also called the Akashic Records. Ether is that "prime matter" in which everything that has ever lived is stored. In old esoteric books the etheric dimension is pictured as a sandy desert furrowed with the tracks of all past epochs, and of each past human life. The Moon-Node horoscope records these "footprints in the sand."

In her *Treatise on Cosmic Fire* Alice Bailey describes the ether as Akasha:

> On the highest plane the combination of these three factors (active heat, latent heat and the primordial substance which they animate) is known as the "sea of fire," of which akasha is the first manifestation of pregenetic matter. Akasha, in manifestation, expresses itself as Fohat, or divine Energy, and Fohat on the different planes is known as aether, air, fire, water, electricity, ether, prana and similar terms. It is the sumtotal of that which is active, animated, or vitalized, and of all that concerns itself with the adaption of the forms to the needs of the inner flame of life.[2]

Today, even modern science is researching the etheric world under the guise of the world of energies. Physicists and astronomers point out that the universe is permeated by electromagnetic currents and fields which are in continual motion and convey uninterrupted "information." Biologists and physicians have investigated the key position held by electromagnetic phenomena in the animal kingdom, as well as in the human nervous system, and in cerebral activity. The inner pulsating forces and the structures of apparently inanimate matter were revealed for the first time by the electron microscope. A fund of experimental knowledge of the micro-world of atomic physics has been amassed, and has been interpreted by theorists employing the concepts of quanta, hypothetical elementary particles, and

---

[2]Alice A. Bailey, *A Treatise on Cosmic Fire* (New York: Lucis, 1951), pp. 43–44.

quarks, to probe more deeply into the hidden fine structure of the universe. The relationships between energy and matter, between order and "chaos" are beginning to make sense, and many of the pronouncements of modern scientists seem, to the lay person, to be remarkably similar to the "ancient" lore of occultists and philosophers. The holistic view of the world will be increasingly recognized as true.

The way in which modern science has been developing is a good example of the fact that scientific knowledge enables us to discover more and more about what underlies our existence. What was earlier concealed, mysterious, and esoteric, and incapable of being understood by ordinary mortals, is being made more accessible to us by this means. Nowadays we experience much that is recondite, but in such a matter-of-fact scientific way that we tend to forget that what is now lit up by conscious understanding and is no longer occult was once a mystery.

Think, for example, of computer technology, in which clever programming and ultra-rapid processing of information remove the need for tedious calculations on paper. It is not farfetched to compare the programming of a computer to the Moon-Node horoscope. If the Moon-Node horoscope does contain a summary of all incarnation experiences, it is actually like a computer, which stores everything that has been programmed into it. And the Node line can be seen as the "code" that makes it possible to enter information into the Moon-Node horoscope. Another approach to this theme is esoteric anatomy, which enables us to form a fair idea of how the Moon-Node horoscope reflects the evolutionary process.

The Four Subtle Bodies of the Human Being

In figure 12 (page 134) an attempt has been made to represent the esoteric constitution of the human being. As will be seen, the etheric body is next to the physical body, then comes the emotional or astral body, and outside this is the mental body, which is enveloped

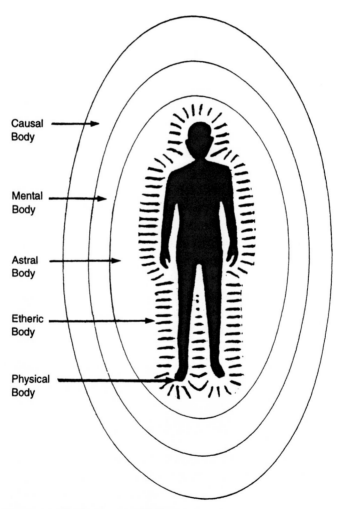

Causal
Body

Mental
Body

Astral
Body

Etheric
Body

Physical
Body

Figure 12. The human constitution.

in turn by the causal body. Not shown in the picture, but also present, are the seven etheric centers, chakras, or lotus blooms.

1. The Etheric Body

Esoteric doctrine implies that the vitality of the human body is derived from the subtle etheric region. The body on its own, without ether, is dead matter—a corpse. At death, the etheric, or vital body separates from the physical body and returns to the planetary ether from which it came, while the physical body descends into the Earth. The etheric body is a little larger than the physical and, throughout life, it supplies all the earthly organs with a flow of vitality. Astrologically the vital body is ruled by Saturn.

2. The Astral Body

The etheric body draws its energy from the so-called astral, or emotional body, the source of every feeling—from anger through devoted love. The astral body, itself, corresponds to the lunar sphere, and the Moon-Node horoscope reflects the contents of this body. Here the polarities and opposites come into play—love and hate, ebb and flow, good and evil—alternating in a rhythm as perpetual as the pulse of life. The astrological ruler of the emotional body is the Moon.

3. The Mental Body

The astral body is embedded in the mental body, which is even more finely structured and flows through everything coarser than itself. The thought processes take place in it, and it emits and receives mental currents. Knowledge accumulates in the mental body and, through a continual learning process, the individual frees himself or herself from the duality and susceptibility to delusion inherent in the astral body. The necessary intelligence is developed by active thinking, because, by differentiating, impartial thought is learned and a greater understanding is gained of the cosmic laws of life in the light of evolutionary theory. The mental body's capacity for thought and judgment is represented by the Sun.

4. The Causal Body

Behind the three bodies just mentioned lies the immutable and deathless self (symbolized by the empty circle in the middle of the birth chart). All the emotional and mental experiences undergone on Earth are sorted out here and treasured up as essence, life quality, or life motivation. It is the causal body that is involved in a continual exchange of information with the so-called Akashic Records, which the clairvoyant reads to ascertain something about the past or future of a client. Each life lived by an individual is processed on the causal plane, and its essence is extracted and stored in the form of empirical values.

At the end of life, the contents of the causal body can be represented by some geometrical figure. We know that the configurations in the horoscope are symbolic lines portraying the geometry and structure of the individual consciousness. Looked at in this way, the aspect picture can be said to mirror the causal body, and it gives us a geometrical epitome of all our former deeds and accomplishments in a mode that can be read and interpreted. Usually, the situation of the aspect picture in the Moon-Node horoscope differs from that in the radix; and we infer from the displacement of houses that a dynamics of development is at work, which compels us to adapt and learn.

Example: If the center of gravity of the planets and of the aspect picture lies on the "I"-side of the Moon-Node horoscope, we can conclude that in former lives ego-development stood in the foreground. Now if the aspect picture is shifted to the "You"-side in the radix, then the native must draw back from the obsession with self and must learn to serve—as efficiently as possible—a partner or group.

Esoteric Definition of the Moon's Node

If we wish to understand the full significance of the Moon-Node horoscope, we shall need some background knowledge concerning the constitution of the human being; in particular, a knowledge of the doctrines of evolution and reincarnation (or rebirth). From the point of view of reincarnation, the Moon-Node horoscope gives a summary of all experiences in former lives, and carries a charge of unconscious knowledge in the form of lessons learned in the course of evolution. What is more, all unresolved conflicts from the past are stored in the MNH, together with tasks left undone which have given us unconscious guilt feelings. The latter can become quite unsettling, and even tormenting, during transits of the Age Point or of other AP-aspects.

We shall consider the Moon-Node horoscope from three angles:

1. As a storage place for experiences belonging to past lives (inner potential);

2. As a karmic resonance apparatus (the law of cause and effect);

3. As the shadow personality (the unconscious).

In our esoteric definition of the Moon-Node horoscope, we treat it as the depiction of—or rather as a storage place for—the things experienced in past lives. It is comparable to the Akashic Records, that book full of secrets, or the unknown region in the etheric body of our planet where everything that has ever been thought, done, or wished, is registered. The Moon-Node horoscope does not show single deeds (good or bad) performed in past lives, not even those done in the life before this. It shows the energy patterns, the essences or qualities, resulting from the summing up of all previous experiences. These can now be felt only as an essential inner potential, as a positive life program and life quality, or, on the other hand, as compulsive behavior. For the most part, the

MNH exhibits contents of the unconscious: things that, in the course of our development, we have already acquired or achieved to our joy and satisfaction—but also things that gave us trouble, and brought us reverses, defeats, harm, and grief.

From an evolutionary standpoint, it can be seen as the horoscope of our attainments and inner potential. What we have once consciously lived through and assimilated remains available to us as "know-how," as inner knowledge, as something that is consciously usable. We can draw inspiration or take advice from it. In people who live with awareness it is conscience, an inner voice, instinct, or guide; in others, it is an indefinable something that creates anxiety because it cannot be understood. They repress the contents of the Moon-Node horoscope as much as they can, and it becomes their unacceptable part, the shadow personality, on which everything evil can be projected.

Immortality

To understand the Moon-Node horoscope in greater depth, we need to consider the immortality of the soul. It is the soul, or undying spirit, that continues to reincarnate. And it is the soul that hoards that sum of all experiences; for, after death, each of the bodies (even the subtle ones) return to the *materia prima*. The soul is that innermost being that survives when everything else is destroyed. The doctrine of immortality occurs in all the world religions. Of course, it assumes many forms. The form in which we are interested postulates that the life inside us is imperishable and not subject to death, and that only the vessel, the physical body, succumbs to the laws governing matter and then dies. The spirit, the soul, or self, persists forever; and, in keeping with the cosmic laws of rebirth, incarnates in human shape again and again on Earth, in order to achieve a comprehensive consciousness of itself and of the whole universe.

The Law of Evolution

The law of evolution is an essential component of esoteric thought. In esotericism, evolution is regarded as a great process of development involving the entire human race; starting in the hoary past and still proceeding to an unknown goal in the far distant future. The evolutionary hypothesis proposes that a scheme of evolution underlies the whole of creation, and that the human soul or spirit has descended out of the pure divine consciousness into matter in order to manifest itself in physical form. The soul is sheathed in a succession of new forms for the purpose of perfecting itself. According to the doctrine of reincarnation and to esoteric astrology, the soul itself chooses both its time of birth and the family providing the most suitable conditions for its further development, so that it can grow inwardly and deal with guilt, or make amends in some way—perhaps in a parental role or by putting up with difficult brothers and sisters, etc.

Meanwhile, the soul is anchored to eternity and shares in the whole history of evolution.

If we become spiritually aware, we shall live with our consciousness outside time and have an overview of each separate life within the wider framework. Many unnecessary cares with which we have weighed ourselves down will automatically disappear. We shall realize that what we are today is merely a fraction of the immense sum of our experiences in countless incarnations in the course of human history. Where we find ourselves in the next life will depend on the stage of development reached in this one.

The Doctrine of Reincarnation

The idea of development underlies astrological psychology; therefore it is understandable that the doctrine of reincarnation appeals to us. It seems so clear that we have lived more than once and that we shall live repeatedly until we have reached our goal.

This is hard for materialists to comprehend; their minds reject the concept that they have lived before. They believe that "new-ageism" is misleading. But we think they are cutting themselves off from the experiences recorded in their unconscious. Due to a vague sense of anxiety, they are keeping their unconscious under lock and key. They energetically oppose fresh ideas and take pains to cover their own depths. Apparently they do not realize that by doing so they are deceiving themselves and hindering their development. The part of themselves they have repressed will play havoc with their lives until it is brought out into the light of everyday consciousness; or, in other words, until they have come to grips with it—and for this the Moon-Node horoscope is outstandingly helpful.

Reincarnation Therapy

Even modern psychology is now prepared to consider the possibility that the roots of psychological disorders are to be found in past lives. Many practitioners are using "reincarnation therapies" in an endeavor to make their patients recall these past lives; the idea being to conquer the past and to reprocess suppressed materials. In reincarnation therapy, the analysis of the past is pursued not only into early childhood but beyond the time of conception and into earlier lives, that is to say into a measureless field of activity. Instead of the rather dubious techniques of hypnosis and self-hypnosis favored not so long ago, people are now trying guided imagination or controlled dreams, mood music, and relaxation, so that internal images can enter consciousness and be interpreted as memories of past lives.

Thus they are attempting to bring their repressions back into consciousness in order to be set free from powerful complexes (or from karma). Rebirth and reincarnation are popular themes today, and the media have latched onto them. It has been determined from a statistical poll that already 8–10 percent of German-speaking people think it may be possible that they have lived once before. "What mystic circles formerly guarded as a hidden treasure, is now common currency," exclaims a psychological magazine. The longterm aim is a new "unity of thought and feeling, of understanding and intuition, of soul and body, of the individual and the world, a unity of all our lives from beginning to end, and indeed a unity with the cosmos itself from which each individual "I" has proceeded—and to which it must one day return."

Always Another Chance

For those who are interested in further progress and want to do something positive with their lives, it is liberating to know that they will have repeated opportunities to improve and to correct faulty development. It will be obvious to them that the goal of development can never be reached in a single lifetime, but takes many lifetimes and a very long period amounting, perhaps, to millions of years. Exactly how many millions, nobody knows, but long enough to provide us with a repeated opportunity to incarnate. In each life we have the chance to develop further and to approach a little nearer to our goal; all the difficulties and problems we have to overcome are there so that we can climb a stage higher. It is a comforting thought that we have such a long time in which to incarnate and that we can do so often until we attain the desired perfection. This way of looking at things gives us a new feeling for time, for cycles, phases of development and growth processes, and also for the regulatory and healing laws of the universe.

Integration

Having used the word "perfection," we should perhaps say that, in the opinion of C. G. Jung, it might be better to speak of "integra-

tion," because we can work on our integration, whereas perfection
lies too far off, and from the point of view of the present is a mere
abstraction. The notion of integration involves a belief in some
dynamic force that underlies the events of development, produc-
ing our life or fate, as the case may be, and continually adjusting
and improving us until we have reached the necessary wholeness.
If we are harmoniously integrated into the stream of development, we find it relatively easy to do everything that helps to make
us better beings. There are laws of balance in our nature which
can mean that what has been overdeveloped in a former life is
reduced in this life, and what has been underdeveloped will be
encouraged to grow by the demands of our environment. The reg-
ulating principles concerned are called "compensatory processes"
in astrological psychology.

Release from Guilt

On putting the Moon-Node horoscope in this broad framework
of the compensatory principle, we set aside the question of guilt.
The word guilt has been much misused and clogs the construc-
tive and liberating activity of our souls. As already said, we should
learn to cast our eye over the Moon-Node horoscope not to
attach praise or blame, but to see the potentials and achievements hidden in its "treasure chest" that awaits discovery by the
conscious mind.

If we look at our life from this vantage point, it will unfold in
its entirety as a more meaningful learning process. By accepting
life's significance, we can free ourselves from remorse and tune
into divine love. It is the old mystery of the universal love known
as grace, which helps us to accept our lot gladly and confidently
and thus to activate inner healing forces. Not infrequently, when
we make "soul contact" in this way, we suddenly lose our guilt feelings in an inrush of wound-healing energies. If it turns out that
everything in which we are involved is as it should be, the fear van-

ishes. We can give it our assent if it is governed by the dynamics of development and is liable to make us more complete, to integrate us, and to adjust the faulty development in our personality. Whatever appears in the horoscope makes a symbolic reference to our further progress. This is the basic idea found in the Moon-Node horoscope when it is treated as the summation of all our experiences in former lives and compared with the radix and the house horoscope. If we latch onto it, it will save us from the snare of the black-and-white thinking that misses the overall significance of things and plays down the value of the forces of love.

Historical Awareness

An additional important increase in awareness takes place when we take history into account. On our long road of development we must surely have found ourselves in many different societies. Yet it is very noticeable that those who have a keen interest in reincarnation discover a preference for specific cultures. In fact, they seem to be beguiled by just one cultural milieu. Many, for example, are captivated by the times of ancient Egypt or ancient Greece, others feel drawn to India, China, or Russia, or to the life of Native Americans. Others, as they practice visualization, conjure up scenes from the Middle Ages and see themselves in cloisters—or they may seem to be transported to the Roman Empire, to the Victorian Age, or to the settlements of the Pilgrim Fathers of the United States. In order to come to terms with the unconscious contents of the Moon-Node horoscope, it is good to explore and discriminate affinities such as these.

Karma and Dharma

Another consideration is the law of karma. It is the law of cause and effect, and is very widely known in the West today. It operates to preserve a balance: "As you sow, so shall you reap." Dharma, on the other hand, is a creative process involving the mastery of life through intelligence. According to the law of karma there is nothing a person thinks, does, or wishes, that does not enter the great energy pool of the cosmos in order to come back to that person one day. Former errors return as blows of fate which have to be endured and lived down until enough sagacity has been developed to produce balance and harmony.

A comprehension of karmic law provides a satisfying answer to the questions: from where do I come, why was I born, what is the purpose of my life, why must I suffer this hard lot, and why do others have an easier time than I have? Another point that concerns us here is the question of debt and reparation. Whoever consciously understands this law will perceive that life as it really is has to be accepted as a serious task, and that the responsibility for the unfolding of one's destiny can and must be accepted by each one—not with feelings of being paid back, but in a healthy insightful way.

Anyone who persistently projects miseries and shortcomings on the environment and sees imaginary foes there, wrongly blaming others for personal failures, will cease developing, and will continue to be surrounded by difficult circumstances until able to recognize that everything negative has its roots in the self. "As within, so without" is the first insight needed to transmute karma into dharma. An old piece of wisdom says that the outer world is nought but a mirror of thine inner world. First put thyself in order, activate the good in thee, get in touch with thine inner promise, and with thine immortal self, then wilt thou liberate thyself—by thy growing powers of discernment, by thy sense of responsibility, and by thine intelligence.

This stage of development is reached little by little, it is not there from the start. It will be observed that the law of karma operates, first and foremost, on the unconscious level as the law of guilt and expiation, of punishment and reward, and is accepted as a lesson to be learned only at a more conscious stage, from which dharma arises. According to the wisdom teaching of the Orient,

karma always has a twofold action: firstly, the individual is compelled to pay the debts incurred in former lives and, secondly, he
or she learns to stop doing certain things, knowing that they have
undesirable effects. In this way, he or she creates a better "karma,"
which is known as *dharma* in Indian philosophy.

It follows that dharma develops only when there is awareness,
and when intelligence, powers of discrimination, and a free exercise of the will, are present. Only then does the individual become
creative and able to shape his or her own world. To the degree
that one behaves responsibly and with intelligent discrimination,
one frees oneself from past errors and works towards a better
future. Moreover, one learns to fit into the community as part of
the whole and to act in unison with the cosmic forces. The latter
is the privilege of the fully conscious, individuated human being.
A person who is at one with himself or herself comes in contact
with cosmic energies and with the transforming forces of the self;
and, that being so, everything changes around him or her. Modern astrology is a pointer in this direction.

The Shadow

The Moon-Node horoscope touches, among other things, on the
subject of the shadow. In the teachings of depth psychology, this
is an invisible part of our being which holds drives, wishes, and
projections that are inaccessible to everyday consciousness. These
are things that we usually repress because in normal waking life
they seem to be unsuitable or even dangerous. Therefore the
shadow is frequently seen as negative or "dark." (Of course, it also
has positive contents, just as there is such a thing as good karma.)
Thus, spiritual tendencies can be totally suppressed because they
are not in accord with our dogmatic thinking, or because they
strike us as old-fashioned. These characteristic features remain
unlived although they are part of our personality. "New age" reincarnation therapy deals with such contents; under regression

these become conscious and exhibit causes that can explain the acausal.

C. G. Jung speaks of the "shadow" and regards it as an area of the unconscious that is very hard to access, having been researched so far only by depth psychology. He compares human consciousness to the tip of an iceberg sticking out of the water—the unconscious he symbolizes as the submerged mass of ice, containing both the collective unconscious and the individual conscious, the so-called shadow personality. The latter is the shadow side of our being, in which everything we have been and experienced is stored. It contains our secret desires, and resolved and unresolved psychic problems from the past. Motivations, repressed complexes and guilt feelings are to be found in it, although usually we are unaware of them and cannot even visualize them, let alone admit them. If at all, they emerge in our dreams; yet, believe it or not, they do exercise an influence on our lives—although, in the main, we do not connect them with ourselves but project them on the environment, where they manifest and return to us as fate.

And so, whenever we cannot bear the idiosyncrasies, habits, or characteristics of others, but are sorely tried and irritated by them, we may be sure that part of our own shadow is involved. This means that we have repressed these peculiarities within ourselves. Many an external situation to which we are unavoidably exposed is no more than a reflection of what is within us. We cannot deal with it as long as we regard it as exterior and nothing to do with us. Usually the consequences of these shadow functions are beyond our control. In a measure, they represent deterministic tendencies, things that are done automatically, or psychic compulsion mechanisms, and we are at their mercy. As a rule, we have to suffer them as negative experiences before we see the connection between them and ourselves.

But now, with the help of the latest methods of interpretation, and using the Moon-Node horoscope, we can consciously accept this repressed side of our being. By recognizing that this side also belongs to us, we initiate the work of integration. In other words, there is a horizontal identification which has the motto, "As within, so without," directly comparable with the vertical, "As above, so below." Only when we lay claim to both parts of our estate, can we talk of achieving wholeness.

Mirror Sphere

The theme of reflection, too, is part of the esoteric picture of the world. Thus, the Moon-Node horoscope symbolizes the astral world, that mirror sphere in which our motivations, wishes, and deeds are projected by certain instants of the past (our karma) into the present. In order to enter this unconscious area, we step over the nodal line, which reflects everything like the surface of a glass: inner and outer, above and below.

When we enter the mirror sphere of the shadow, we must be clear in our minds that the law of reflection holds good in this region. We are in the Moon plane, which reflects from various facets everything that comes in contact with it. Many contradictions can be discovered in it. Things which have nothing to do with selfhood, but relate to other people or to the collective unconscious, are here, too. There is a risk that we shall perceive distorted images of impressions, encounters, or experiences, as if in a fairground mirror, and we may be misled by our perceptions. This sphere of deception and illusion, of infatuation with the world, draws us in if we are not careful. There are ancient archetypes in this "underworld." It is the world of demons and phantoms, a battlefield for God and the Devil. It is also the plane of antitheses, of dualities or polarities. We can be swung, as if on a pendulum, from side to side, and (to change the metaphor) may find it almost impossible to thread our way out of the labyrinth. Anyone who enters the Moon's Node plane simply to ferret out the dark forces of the "I" in order to remove or eradicate them, will evoke spirits that may refuse to depart.

Reversal

Reflection always produces a reversal. We all know how quickly one emotion can flip over into its opposite. Intense love can be replaced by equally intense hatred, the hero can become the villain, and *vice versa*. Also accomplishments and noble qualities belonging to the past can become negative, and can hinder our development if they harden into rigid structures. There is an Indian proverb about the conversion of values that says, "Virtue turns into vice." For example, a celibate existence in a cloister can devitalize the etheric body, so that the balance has to be restored by active sexuality in the next life. Quite often, we find in the Moon-Node horoscope the exact opposite of our expectations. What would be good for our personality—for "little me"—can be bad for our soul, and what is good for our soul usually involves a neglect of, or a reenunciation of, the "I." This reversal, or turn through 180 degrees, is the key to correct interpretation of the Moon-Node horoscope. We shall come back to this topic later.

Beyond Good and Evil

In any case, it is very important, when looking at the Moon-Node horoscope to do so objectively without thinking in terms of black and white. Figuratively speaking, we must position ourselves in the middle of the seesaw where we shall not be swayed by either polarity. Here we can find our balance and can control the ups and downs. We shall see the Moon-Node horoscope with new eyes, and examine it in an unprejudiced, neutral, or scientific way. To avoid value judgments, both poles have to be known and accepted as real forces—in a unity of opposites. As long as the accent is on good and evil, crime and punishment, or on reprisals, we live in polarities. Thesis will be confronted by antithesis from time to time, but their synthesis will merely represent the next stage of development.

The Theory of Relativity

In the present century, our thinking has been greatly expanded by Albert Einstein's theory of relativity. This theory has borne fruit not only in physics, but also in philosophy and psychology. By resorting to the relativizing principle, which presents a reasonable and understandable point of view, the either-or thinking of the Middle Ages can be circumvented. Today, everyone knows that a thing has not only two, but many, sides. With the new relativistic mode of thought, we recognize the intermediate tones, the nuances, the niceties. Only by making use of it can we match psychological with esoteric trains of thought. The resolution of the tension between good and evil, between sin and expiation, between thesis and antithesis, and the formation of their synthesis, has long been known as a dialectical method in Western philosophy (cf. the Hegelian Dialectic). Only in the synthesis does one gain knowledge of a higher sort, leaving the plane of opposed polarities, and rising another degree to the plane of "pure reason" and a more coherent understanding. This deeper understanding has always had an evolutionary character.

Synthesis and Making Sense

Making sense and making a synthesis are our deepest concerns when treating three-dimensionality as a complex unity and forming a proper view of the Moon-Node horoscope. As already mentioned, it is axiomatic that we cannot enter the shadow sphere of the past without hurting ourselves unless we are "pure in heart," i.e., unless we avoid premeditating and making value judgments. Whoever, in stepping beyond good and evil, shines a discerning light into the dark places and does not jump to conclusions, will find a doorway in the soul that opens on coherent understanding. Then there will no longer be any talk of good luck and bad luck. Good luck is something one can make for oneself, and bad luck is something one can learn to avoid. Each difficulty is overcome by knowing that it brings us a little further forward in our development. Then each problem, and even each defeat, loses its horrible paralyzing effect. Everything depends on interpretation and awareness.

Integration of the Shadow

When we see the Moon-Node horoscope as the sum total of our life history in the evolutionary process and as a store of experience and potential, then we can integrate our "shadow" (as we should wish to do, since it contains things that are latent abilities). If we regard the shadow as evil, we can hardly love it, but will treat it as infernal and blame it all over again, even though the evil may have been atoned for long ago. Possibly it is hard to accept that we ought to learn to love our shadow. We love only what appeals to us as worth loving, what helps us on our way, what does us good. But let us remember how much always depends on our awareness. According to the way in which we approach the shadow, so it shows itself to us. Think of the law of reflection, or of the well-known proverb: "Whatever you shout into the wood, the wood shouts back." We ourselves are called upon to rescue our shadow by giving it its true significance. Released from guilt, we can accept the forces, the experiences, and the essences of the shadow as an integral part of ourselves. But, before we reach this stage, we must be capable of thinking through the consequences of our actions, and must also be prepared to bear the total responsibility for whatever we do.

According to depth psychology, everything a person cannot endure in someone else is a repressed part of himself or herself. Whatever is not being lived will continue to be projected on others for as long as it is not being dealt with. Consciously dealing with it, which helps to integrate the shadow, can be made considerably easier by referring to the Moon-Node horoscope. Acceptance of the fact that external events mirror internal events produces great changes. If one recognizes oneself as the instigating "I," one will realize one's creative potential, and one's inner ability to improve one's life and fate. Then one will no longer wait for assistance from outside, but will rely on self-help and will unremittingly pursue further development through creative consciousness.

Psychological Methods

Some schools of psychology undertake a script analysis of the effects of impressions in the unconscious. Of course, they look for a "script" consisting of behavioral patterns imprinted by the milieu now, and take no account of former lives; but we can use script analysis to reconstruct imprints that relate to the Moon-Node horoscope.

Say, for the sake of argument, we spent a former life in a monastery or convent. The strictly regulated daily routine, with early rising, prayers, and religious rites, was so often repeated (perhaps for fifty, sixty, or more years), that we can speak of a "script." I like to think of it as a "fixed track" to which a person's movements are confined. And this is one explanation for psychological compulsions or, in esoteric terms, karma. We keep falling back into the old patterns of behavior, often without realizing it.

Most people assume that they are responsible only for those actions that they have done deliberately. They do not bear in mind that they will also be called to account for their unconscious actions.

But, time and again, we can unintentionally get into situations in which we react wrongly. Situations which leave us unable to say why we behaved or spoke as we did, and yet we are left to pick up the pieces. So often, impulses from the unconscious push us into doing something we really have no wish to do. These are psychic compulsion mechanisms, repressions, or karmic causes.

Chapter 2

Reincarnation and
the Archetypes

What are Archetypes? • Reminiscences • Prominent
Structures • Historical Characters • Triggers • The State of
Forgetting • The Consultation • Stimulus Words • The
Archetypes • Adventurer, Artist, Sailor • Materialist • Cultural
Level and Education • Power Structures and
Aristocracy • Ecclesiastical Background • Monastic Life •

What are Archetypes?

To see how the key concept "reincarnation archetype" works, we need to be clear about its meaning. By archetype we understand a primordial image initially imprinted in living matter. Biology itself adopts this definition when it envisages the "basic model of a species of animal as a reconstruction of the formative principle contained in a primary pattern enshrining the ancestral history." Similarly, the psychology of C. G. Jung deems archetypal any inherited component of the collective unconscious that serves as a base for the personality structure. Thus "archetypal" means "corresponding to a primal form."

In our view, this primal form has arisen in the course of many incarnations of the soul. Religions speak of incarnation (Christ in John 1: 14) and of reincarnation (Buddha); also some of the old philosophers refer to reincarnation or the re-embodiment of the soul. The principle of "re-incarnation" (or the repeated post-mortem entry of the soul into new bodies to continue a tremendously long learning process that is part of the history of our race) must be grasped before we can go on to discuss such things as reincarnation archetypes.

The latter are patterns of human behavior that have arisen in history, in the wake of the various cultural, religious, and linguistic stages of development. Role models have come into being in this way and have been handed down to us (among other things in literature), and everyone seems to have a familiarity with them.

Some individuals feel this familiarity more strongly than others. They know about these archetypal roles not only from what they have learned from others but from what they have picked up with their own personal antennae. An archetypal role will suddenly emerge as a memory of a former life, or perhaps something else will put them on its trail. Many folk experience flashbacks to previous incarnations; as when, for example, they are in some city they have never visited before and find it strangely familiar. In the depths of the psyche, images of past lives are resting, ready to be raised into consciousness by so-called triggers. These triggers can be personal encounters, the hearing of a piece of music, or the sight of a historical monument such as the Great Pyramid, the Tower of London, or Stonehenge, etc.

Reminiscences

Many reports have come from people who, let us say, were strolling in Florence beside the river Arno when they suddenly had the feeling of being transported to another era. The impression they received was that they had lived there before. In the same way, there are those who are irresistibly attracted to the age of the Pharaohs, or of the Aztecs or Incas, or of the old Chinese or Buddhist civilizations. They feel sure that they once belonged to those periods. Indeed, any of us can visualize human history as a parade of civilizations marching past the inner eye, and can quietly observe which of them evoke images that seem to come from our own past and which do not. The vague sense of recognition of a certain culture or person is the first indication of a genuine memory of a former life.

Prominent Structures

The Moon-Node horoscope, too, helps us to remember. As already said, it admits us to the deepest layers of our beings, where the knowledge of the past is stored. However, we should note that we shall not find in the Moon-Node horoscope personal particulars such as profession, rank, name, and place of residence, but only prominent structures indicating typical attitudes and modes of behavior, which we shall call "reincarnation archetypes" in what follows. Thus what are shown in the Moon's Node are not single lives, but deep-lying patterns of behavior which have persisted over several lives.

If, say, one has been shut away in a cloister for fifty years, a religious attitude will have developed and will have imprinted a permanent character trait. When someone spends fifty years expressing an intense yearning for God in daily prayer, it is natural to suppose that a fixed structure of religiosity will be left in that person's psyche. Again, if someone spends a life in poverty and in a struggle for existence, then either that person will remain in constant fear of going without, or will develop the character trait of self-denial, being satisfied with very little and prepared to cope with tough conditions.

Such ingrained character traits and modes of behavior are like an internal template for living. They rule the present from the past, are translated into flesh and blood, and reveal (in addition to an inner potential or capacity) psychic compulsion mechanisms and set ways—or "fixed tracks." From an esoteric point of view, they represent a person's karma.

Historical Figures

If we accept that the Moon-Node horoscope shows the sum of the life experiences of earlier incarnations, the question arises as to how this knowledge can be made available to our everyday consciousness. Are there special methods and possibilities for activating the hidden information?

As mentioned above, the Moon-Node horoscope (just like the radix) does not supply biographies, but only leading structures of an archetypal character. It is relatively easy to show its nature by referring to historical figures. If, for example, we find a power structure (4/10-tension) in the Moon-Node horoscope, we immediately call to mind Caesar or Napoleon.

A man who tends to impose his will on others may well be called Napoleonic. Someone who champions the poor and the oppressed can be compared to Robin Hood. Someone else, who defends an ideal with all his might, and fights for it in spite of mockery and persecution, is said to have a crusader mentality (both types of behavior are chiefly aligned with the 5/11 axis). Anyone who is constantly criticizing, condemning, or punishing others, is playing the part of judge (and probably has planets, especially Saturn, in the 8th or 9th house). And if he or she carries out cruel persecution in the name of God, we think of the inquisitors (3/9 tension).

When we look back on such historical phenomena as the Inquisition, horrifying as they are today, we need to remember the mental level of the majority of people living at the times in question. They sought to justify to themselves many of the deeds that make us shudder now, and even called them necessary. Often we can penetrate their motives by allowing for what they knew. We, too, in former existences were tied to the destiny of the group, and while wishing to do good may have become agents of evil.

We should guard against being too quick to judge and condemn, especially when counselling. This also applies when historical figures fascinate the native. Many times these figures have so powerful an effect that clients identify with them and are firmly convinced that they themselves were once Napoleon, Columbus, or Marie-Antoinette. This is nearly always a delusion, and often a sign of mental illness. All that can truthfully be said is that in their shadow personalities they have certain things (e.g., reactions or motivations) in common with these figures.

Triggers

Our unconscious is full of features that are characteristic of such archetypes. In a psychological interpretation they are frequently called pseudo-personalities or partial personalities. It is well known that the experiences, achievements, or partial personalities lying dormant in the unconscious can be activated and made conscious by the right stimulus. Psychosynthesis works, for example, with exercises in guided imagination; psychoanalysis uses (among other things) the interpretation of dreams; reincarnation therapy deals with the life of the imagination. In astrologo-psychological consultancy, a single stimulus word is often enough to initiate this process of becoming conscious. The stimulus word triggers the memory, and brings back experiences that had slipped into oblivion.

The State of Forgetting

Even if we knew every detail of our former lives, that would not guarantee a carefree further development. In fact, it makes sense that we have forgotten our previous incarnations. The knowledge of them is not revealed until a certain degree of maturity is attained. Usually the spiritual development of the person determines what memories (if any) of past lives there will be: consequently these ought not to be forced. In the course of evolution, the veil of forgetfulness between separate lives has apparently lifted. In our own day and age, in which so many veils seem to have been torn away, far more people have gained access to former lives and to the hidden treasures of the past. Previously it was, for the most part, only initiates who were introduced to this hidden knowledge. It is interesting, too, that even the knowledge concerning the Moon-Node horoscope can be made generally known now.

There is a great deal of historical evidence to show that true knowledge creates problems for those who try to disseminate it at the wrong time. They lay themselves open to anything from scornful laughter through murderous persecution and suppression.

Today the attitude has altered in many parts of the world. With a change in the consciousness of so many people, the knowledge enshrined in the Moon-Node horoscope can be both necessary and helpful.

The Consultation

The more experience we have with the Moon-Node horoscope, the easier it is to find the right stimulus word for archetypal qualities present in clients. The latter's response will show if we have struck a chord or, to put in it another way, if we have made contact with the inner world of imagery. When the correct archetypical stimulus word has been found, it serves as an "open sesame" that magically unseals the cave and allows the unconscious to be ransacked. It is up to us to find this mystic word; therefore we as counselors need to be able to seize on and describe reincarnation archetypes intuitively with the help of the Moon-Node horoscope. What is more, we need to observe the client's reaction with sensitivity and freedom from prejudice, and to avoid using stimulus words to evoke some reincarnation archetype that, in our private opinion, ought to make its appearance. Intuition ceases to operate as soon as the issue is forced. It is impossible to delve into the deeper layers of the mind without empathy or intuitive understanding. If these are lacking, it is better to defer the consultation until conditions are right.

Stimulus Words

Over a period of many years as a consultant and teacher, I have compiled a list of archetypal stimulus words that have shown themselves to be particularly effective in unlocking the unconscious. What is more, I have attempted to fashion them into a system that could be implemented by others. Due to the great number of possibilities, this has been no easy matter. Naturally, I started with the twelve houses. (In this connection, please re-read the chapter on "The Moon's Node in the Houses" in the first part of this book.) In practice, it was found that the house positions alone do not lead to the right stimulus word.

If we want to run through the archetypal figures systematically, we can start with the temperaments. There are earth, water, air, and fire archetypes; but the three crosses, too (cardinal, fixed, and mutable), have an archetypal character. In my experience, when working with the Moon-Node horoscope, we must always combine different elements in order to discover the individual reincarnation archetypes. In addition, it is indispensable at times to take into account the entire axial theme as well as the aspect picture and the different houses in the Moon-Node horoscope and the natal chart. As is only to be expected, we know conclusively that we have the right word only when the various interpretative elements are made to comply with tried and tested rules.

For the most part, this becomes the creative task of the counselor and therapist; for only in rare horoscopes does the house position lead straight to the correct result. In the following description of the reincarnation archetypes I try, as far as possible, to draw on my own experience. It is for readers themselves to extend this list.

The Archetypes

Adventurer, Artist, Sailor
Fire houses 1, 5, 9
Axis 5/11
In these archetypes, the fire houses are the first to consider. In the 1st house, we are heroes who triumph in all dangers and battles; in the 5th house we are adventurers who shrink from nothing, but

boldly stake all on one venture; in the 9th house we set out toward far horizons in the hope of breaking new ground.

At this point, we should say that the 5/11 axis is the strongest of the archetypal characters, because the fixed axes possess the oldest cultural values. The 5th house always represents the gamester, the adventurer, the risk-taker; the 9th house represents long journeys, the boundless ocean, new lands. Planets in the 5th house very often point to latent creativity, to the artist who lives his or her work and is wholly absorbed in it. A heavily tenanted Moon-Node 5th house suggests the sowing of wild oats, it suggests love and sex, also having children, committing adultery, having casual sex, and supporting or being a mistress. Other possibilities are infanticide and unhappy love affairs. In fact, the 5th house offers a wide range of emotional expressions with, at one extreme a childish faith in love and human goodness and, at the other extreme, a trifling with the affections of others and a refusal to accept obligations. Various sexual manifestations are found here. On the one hand, possessive love, burning jealousy and the elimination of rivals. On the other hand, bashfulness, and the "wall-flower" syndrome, solitary vice, fetishism, exhibitionism, and voyeurism, not to mention obscenity, orgies, crimes of passion, etc.

A Sun in the 5th house keeps on shining in the same old way. The natives have sex appeal; they fascinate others and move through life with charm. With a Sun in the Moon-Node 5th house, they easily gain support, and throw themselves into fresh projects with initiative, enthusiasm, and courage. Not ones to hang around, they take risks, and are ready to try anything once. Intense experiences are like the elixir of life to them and activate their creative force. Life is enjoyed and everything is investigated, whether in erotic or in ordinary journeys of discovery. These folk ought to do something creative today, too, otherwise their practical dynamism will turn inwards and leave them inhibited or neurotic.

Often the archetypical figures that emerge in connection with houses twelve and nine are—in addition to the adventurer, the artist, and the lover—the mariner, the pirate, and the freebooter; possibly the traits of these characters were exhibited in some past seafaring life. Also the freedom yet adherence to custom of the Romanies and other nomads are represented by the 5th house. Such archetypes are shown by combinations, not by a single Moon-Node house.

Archetypical stimulus words for adventurer, artist: The lover, the artist, the seafarer, the knight-errant, the harlot, the prostitute, the mistress, the freebooter, the buccaneer, the pirate, the gypsy or Romany, the eternal wanderer, the nomad, the Gilgamesh syndrome.

Materialist
Earth houses 2, 6, 10
Axis 2/8

Obviously, all earth houses have to do with the material sustenance of life. We may expect to find the hardened materialist in the fixed 2nd house, those who use wealth to acquire power in the 10th, while in the 6th house we encounter those anxieties of everyday life that can draw a person into materialism.

The 2/8 axis is symbolic of that ancient archetype that has shaped the human attitude to possessions ever since the stone age. All manner of means for defending the property of individuals and of tribal communities were developed in the course of thousands of years. Here we find warfare for living space and resources, and the struggle for possessions. When one has too little of these things, they are seized from others.

If the 2/8 axis is occupied by an opposition in the Moon-Node horoscope, this theme is an ingrained pattern of behavior. Countermeasures are taken immediately there is a risk of losing anything. For many, this axis is completely deterministic and it features psychological compulsion mechanisms that ought to be thoroughly researched. Rooted here is a deep dread of having to do without the necessities of life: a dread that often amounts to paranoia. Possibly one has been very poor in a former life, and that is why this axis is so strongly emphasized. Such people hardly ever do something for nothing, they always calculate the profit, and near-ly always get it. They compare themselves with others and complain loudly if anyone receives more than they do. In inheritances, for example, they try to ensure that nobody's bequest is bigger than theirs. There are many forms of behavior in this possession axis, so it is not unlikely that this is the oldest archetype.

Certainly, with this Moon-Node house opposition, it is to be expected that the native will want to have as much as possible of this world's goods in order to enjoy life and to hold on to it. Because of the intense desire to be financially secure, he or she tries to keep everything and part with nothing. Possessions are a ruling passion, as is the accumulation of wealth. Unquestionably, in many of the native's past lives, special attention has been paid to the development of financial ability. Therefore this ability is now present. Almost always there is a gift for making money.

A Sun in the 2nd Moon-Node house gives the underlying conviction that one will always have enough. The native does not worry about cash, because he or she always knows how to obtain it. That is because the Sun is in this house; and wherever the Sun is placed in the Moon-Node horoscope, there we are in control of our lives.

Of course, a 2/8 opposition in the Moon-Node horoscope can also be the symbol of crimes against property, wars of conquest, piracy, and the destruction of foreign possessions. There have been countless wars and battles in the past—enough for the native of a horoscope of this type to have been present at one or more. With placements in the 2nd and 8th houses, we may expect to find the power of the serviceman to defeat the enemy, and the strategic skill of the general. The soldier who followed his king onto the field of battle is a genuine archetypal figure who fits in here. Military life also belongs to the 6/12 axis and to placements of Mars in houses 8 through 12.

From the archetypal standpoint we also call axis 2/8 the "Mafia-axis" when extortion, menaces, and retaliation, are the order of the day. At this stage the law "an eye for an eye, a tooth for a tooth" is in force, along with vendettas, revenge, and retribution. The robber-baron mentality belongs here, too. In some cultures it used to be thought fair game to seize anything that caught one's eye. Only over the centuries have laws safeguarding property developed.

Archetypal stimulus words for materialism: Financial power, the rich, the landowner, banker, merchant, capitalist, war of conquest, robber-baron, thief, hostilities, the soldier, the general, the Mafia, profit and gain, poverty, avarice, fear of starvation, death, loss, reverses, war and destruction.

Cultural level and education

Air houses 3, 7, 11

Predominant axis 3/9

The air houses participate very largely in intellectual cultural development. Usually the 3rd house shows how well we have been educated, and the 11th house shows how highly we rate ourselves. In the 7th house we need a partner to increase our cultural awareness and to give us appreciation.

The certainty of intelligence and possession of necessary knowledge is shown chiefly by major planets in the 3rd house of the Moon-Node horoscope. With the Sun there, these people know just how knowledge can be acquired. Many have good instincts for opportunities—for the right books, and the right teachers; in the present life, they obtain with ease the knowledge they need and can utilize. Others with major planets in this field participate actively in cultural life. They have frequently been teachers or writers, and they possess the ability to make others listen to them for they are good speakers and orators. Often they have no planets in the radical 3rd house and yet they display this ability; then it is the Moon-Node horoscope that discloses the connection with former accomplishments.

What is more, intellectual complexes can be recognized in the Moon-Node horoscope. An opposition on the thought axis 3/9 nearly always shows a one-track mind or a difficulty in thinking which can assume a complex character. There is a tormenting fear of forgetting what one was going to say and of the mind going blank without warning. Planets in the 3rd Moon-Node house may indicate exam nerves, even though there is no such indication in the radix.

Since everything undergoes a 180-degree turn in the Moon-Node horoscope and is shown in reverse (see the earlier chapter on "Mirror Spheres"), an unaspected Mercury in the 3rd house (for example) can indicate illiteracy, possibly through lack of educational opportunities. But it can also indicate the very opposite. Mercury when unaspected, may show itself in its purest form and bestow a bright and artful mind, which puts a spoke in everywhere, does not give a fig for qualifications, is always popping up with something to say, and—need it be said—grates on other people's nerves.

The 11th house is an "aristocratic enclave" in the Moon-Node horoscope. Usually, with the major planets in this house, we belonged to the upper crust, we were highly educated, and maybe sophisticated or a snob. Often this reveals itself in a supercilious attitude toward the less privileged (giving oneself airs, expecting star treatment, being a lounge-lizard). Now if, in the radix, there is nothing special in the 11th house, but the emphasis is switched to the 3rd house, then the native should strive for genuine knowledge, because this side of life is no longer in its infancy. One can no longer count on being respected simply for being born into a cultured aristocratic family. To drive this lesson home, it sometimes happens that one is laughed at for being ignorant or for getting poor grades at school.

If there are several planets in the 7th house of the Moon-Node horoscope, there is nearly always a talent for matters relating to partnership. The native may even be considered a partnership specialist, because of the way he or she has learned to live with close companions over many lives. There is a highly intelligent approach to this theme: the native knows exactly how to secure a partner, and what steps must be taken to find the right one. But if the emphasis lies on the "I"-side rather than on the

"You"-side, then the individual wants nothing more to do with marriage or partnership. Having gone through this a thousand times already, having had "enough" of it, this person will fight hard to save personal freedom.

Archetypal stimulus words for cultural level and education: University, school class, the erudite, professor, arbiter of taste, the arrogant, the snob, the university lecturer, the teacher, parish clerk, author, poet, prose writer, the smart and the dumb, the know-nothing, the know-all, the eternal student, matrimony.

Power Structures and Aristocracy
Houses 8, 9, 10 and 11
Predominant axes 4/10 and 5/11
Major planets in the upper sector of the Moon-Node horoscope usually suggest a personality that at some stage has been able to exercise power: in the 8th house through a judgeship, in the 9th through personal knowledge, in the 10th through high office, and in the 11th through aristocratic status.

Essentially, power structures belong to the cardinal cross, but operate mainly along the vertical axis. In the Moon-Node horoscope they are visible in the 10th house and in the 4/10 opposition. People with 4/10 tension in the Moon-Node horoscope are often allergic to power structures because these suppress their own desire for power. They cannot bear to be bossed about. Many know or suspect that in former lives they have misused power and possibly have been ruined by it; so now they would rather not possess it; consequently they often find themselves pushed into situations where, much to their chagrin they have to do as they are told. If they recognize with the help of the Moon-Node horoscope that what they are doing is stifling their own lust for power, and if they accept it inwardly in a new way and try to integrate it, they can gradually master their fate and liberate themselves from external restraints.

In addition, the 11th house is a very powerful influence in the Moon-Node horoscope. Nearly always it has to do with an aristocratic ancestry, or membership of a prominent power group. Those who have the Sun in this house may have once belonged to the top layer of society or to a very powerful court, order or brotherhood. Even today one can see the duke or baron in the physiognomy of many of these individuals. They identify with such roles, and if the Sun is in the lower sector of the radix they usually feel unappreciated, like Cinderella or monarchs who have been dethroned. This state of mind easily develops into the so-called princess-syndrome, because the native often acts like royalty. But the law of development necessitates that we learn all of life's roles—sometimes being the top dog and at others the underdog.

Archetypal stimulus words for power structures and aristocracy: The dictator, the king, the officer, the autocrat, the knight, the baron, the celebrity, the princess-syndrome (often with the Moon in the 11th house), the deposed king or queen (when the major planets occupy the lower sector of the radix); the quixotic mentality with an opposition on the 5/11 axis, or when spiritual planets show that the native is devoted to a lifelong ideal.

Ecclesiastical Background
Water houses 4, 8, 12
11th and 9th houses, 3/9 opposition
Because the development of the Western world has been strongly influenced by the church over the last two thousand years, memories of past lives often feature ecclesiastical roles. Natives easily identify with the figure of a clergyman, a priest, a cardinal, or a bishop. Houses 9 and 11 are prominent in these archetypal characteristics. An opposition on the thought-axis suggests cooperation with the Inquisition. Perhaps these natives have condemned people to death in the name of God or of some authority (the state, the king, or the pope), have seen themselves as an instrument of divine vengeance, have burnt witches. Of course, in addition to showing up in the 3/9 opposition, these themes usually appear in an occupation of the 11th and 8th houses, too. In the 11th house, rigid dogmatic thought structures are visible, along

with fanaticism and a refusal to compromise; in the 8th house we have the judgment-seat, and the upholding of the law.

Our personal karma is determined by the law of cause and effect; in the Moon-Node horoscope, where karma is recorded, this law always produces a reversal. In other words, if we have misused a judicial office, we ourselves have inevitably met with persecution and condemnation. We have experienced both the one and the other. In the incarnation-archetypes one has been both judge and convict, culprit and victim, robber and robbed, adulterer and cuckold.

With one of the three major planets in the 9th lunar house, one has definitely had to confront questions of religion and of philosophy, too, often in the context of Greek temples or of sacred female dancers. The Sun in this house is always a sign of independent thought; the native seeks a superior viewpoint and a philosophical answer to life. If, in addition, Jupiter is on the MC, a priestly function is obvious. In some way or other the native was a benefactor, and cared for the people in the 4th house. Neptune and Jupiter together in this region of the Moon-Node horoscope are often the sign of a bishop, or possibly a missionary. The native has been thoughtful of others, has preached the Word of God to them, has blessed them, and has tried to bring them salvation. This individual may still long to play such a role again. Quite often this person actually looks like a cleric, even when there is nothing in the radical 9th house. With a little imagination, we can picture this person wearing a cardinal's hat or holding a crosier.

Usually, with Saturn in the 11th Moon-Node house, clerical dogmas or political principles are imposed on others by all possible means. The natives will invariably try to insist on having orders obeyed and requirements fulfilled. This placement of Saturn harks back to the mother superiors who, when they scourged the novices for their sins, did so in the name of the Church—excessive behavior no longer tolerated. It does not take much acumen to realize that nowadays this house placement has lost its effect: it belongs to the past. Today, people do not take kindly to threats of punishment. So now we have to consider the house occupied by

Saturn in the radix, which signifies what lesson has to be learned. We describe this change in values in the chapter on "House Displacement."

Archetypal stimulus words for the ecclesiastical sector: Mother Church, religion, belief, dogma, priesthood, temple dancer, friar or monk, cardinal's hat, crosier, missionary, pope, abbot, abbess, inquisition, heresy, the burning of witches, guilt and atonement, punishment.

Monastic Life
Water houses 4, 8, 12
12th and 9th houses, axis 6/12

If we find planets in the 12th house of the Moon-Node horoscope, we can be sure that the native has spent several lives in seclusion or isolation. This usually means that even in this life, he or she has no objection to being alone and may even feel an inner need for solitude from time to time. With the major planets there, the native must have spent one or more lives in a cloister or on a remote farmstead, or even in prison. The combination with the other houses is significant here. When the 6/12 axis is involved, life has often been Spartan. Perhaps one has not paid much regard to physical existence, and has delegated one's responsibility to Mother Church, especially with Saturn in the 12th or 6th Lunar house. But, in retrogressing, there is a need to distinguish between a Catholic monastery and a lamasery or some other closed order.

With several planets (especially Neptune) in the 12th house, we tend to think of a mystical Christian life of retirement from the world together with celibacy. Uranus and Pluto point more to a Buddhist monastery. Planets in the 11th house also point in this direction. With Saturn posited in the 11th house, monastic life has usually involved a position of authority such as that possessed by an abbot or abbess. In the case of membership of a closed order where the native has lived a life of prayer in total seclusion, the 5th and 8th houses contribute self-mortification mechanisms.

On the 6/12 axis of the Moon-Node horoscope we also encounter the helper syndrome. And if, in addition, Neptune is in the second house, we can speak of a "St. Francis syndrome." The natives will give the shirts off their backs in the spirit of total resignation. They live very modestly, and share what they have with others even though these may possess more than themselves. A typical attitude resulting from previous behavior of this sort is that sacrifices are futile and unnecessary and usually no good to anybody. One must remember that the Moon-Node houses do not apply to the present; they belong to the past and, to that extent, are illusory.

Then again, there are helper and martyr syndromes on this axis. Those with 6/12 tensions in the Moon-Node horoscope and with corresponding planets or configurations in the fixed houses 8 and 11 are always ready to make sacrifices. They want to carry everything unpleasant and all the suffering in the world on their own shoulders, and they take troubles and burdens upon themselves quite needlessly. This behavior can also occur with 2/8 tension, only then the motivation is different. On that fixed axis, one makes sacrifices and practices resignation in the hope of earning a place in heaven.

Archetypal stimulus words for monastic life: Monk, nun, abbot, abbess, novice, the religious, seclusion, isolation, the St. Francis syndrome, the martyr, the ascetic.

Chapter 3

Practical Rules
for Interpretation

Elements of Interpretation • House Displacement • The Aspect
Picture • Vertical and Horizontal Displacement • Example
Horoscope: Stephan • Displacement of Planets • Example
Horoscope: Maria • Displacement of Sun and Moon • Planets
in the Same House • Three-dimensionality • Example
Horoscope: Nora • Sun in the Same House • Further Rules
of Interpretation • Peregrine Planets in the MNH • Secondary
Personalities • Oppositions • The Same Axis • Power Structures •
Moon-Node Age Point • Crossing-points C1 and C2 • Example
Horoscope: Susanne • The Crossing Axis • Age Point Opposition •

Elements of Interpretation

As described in detail in the first part of this book, we can apply all the known elements of interpretation to the Moon-Node horoscope: the classification is the same as in the natal chart. The central circle in the middle is a useful image of the imperishable self or soul. Surrounding this center is the geometrical aspect picture, then come the planets in the signs and in the houses. When examining the aspect picture we can proceed in accordance with the first five rules of interpretation taught in our school. We consider the lie of the aspect picture in the house system, the dynamics, coherence, and color of the aspects, and their vertical or horizontal direction. In the next stage of interpretation, we make a careful study of the three personal planets, the Sun, Moon, and Saturn, because it is our personality that looks for further development.

But now, in addition to the familiar rules, there is the comparison with the radix, which has more to do with house displacement than with the aspect picture and the personal planets. The Low Points shift a little because in the Moon-Node horoscope we are dealing with 30-degree houses. Nevertheless, it has been found that planets near the cusps of the Moon-Node horoscope always have some bearing on the present, whereas those found in the middle region of a house, close to the Low Point, seem to have little significance. However, much depends on the stage of development and degree of maturity reached by the person in question.

House Displacement

The displacement that is apparent when the aspect pictures and the house positions of the radix and of the Moon-Node horoscope are set side by side, is one of the most important elements of interpretation available to us for investigating the developmental dynamics of an individual. If we accept that each individual reincarnates over and over again in order to improve his or her nature and character, then we must also assume that each new incarnation teaches something that will aid further development. Seen in this light, the whole of life is a learning process and everything that happens assists the unfolding of the person's mental and spiritual potential. As already mentioned, this developmental process, this growth and ripening into a complete human being, is regulated by the principle of compensation that underlies the whole of evolution. As applied to our little lives, this can be expressed in the following simple formula:

Whatever we have strongly developed in former lives is deactivated, and whatever we have neglected is activated.

The Aspect Picture

In astrological psychology we can study this dynamics of development by various methods. Apart from dynamic measurement, a comparison of the aspect picture in the two charts (the Moon-Node horoscope and the radix) gives us an insight into this theme. On comparing the two charts, we see immediately the extent to which the aspect picture has been displaced in the house system. We can tell at a glance where the center of gravity of the aspect picture once lay and where it now lies (in the current radix). To help the reader to detect the displacement, we present a simple division of the horoscope into its upper and lower halves and into its right and left halves. As is well known, the left half of the horoscope is the "I"-side and the right half is the "You"-side. Also the lower half represents the unconscious and the upper half the conscious, so that the region above the horizon indicates individual liberties and the region below it indicates dependence on the collective. The upper region has more to do with thought, and the lower region has more to do with action. In this connection, the quadrants are significant too, as may be gathered from looking at figure 13 on page 174.

Vertical and Horizontal Displacement

Just as important as the center of gravity of the aspect picture within the compass of the horoscope, is the general direction of the contours of the aspect picture. If the majority of aspects run vertically, from top to bottom or *vice versa*, we interpret this as signifying individual effort. The native has to develop entirely individually; especially as he or she looks for work that is a true vocation. But if the majority of aspects run horizontally, from left to right or the reverse, we speak of a consciousness that will find expression in the relationship between "I" and "You."

It is interesting to study the two charts (the radix and the Moon-Node horoscope) from this standpoint. If the general direc-

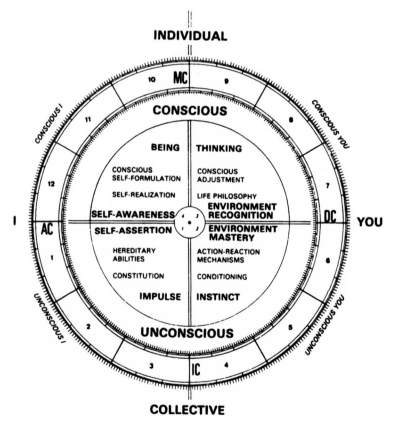

Figure 13. The quadrants.

tion of the aspect picture alters significantly, for example from horizontal to vertical, a transformation of consciousness is required in the present life; this person needs to free himself or herself from "You"-dependency. The tendency to tag along with others is overcome now with the help of a more independent attitude. Usually this happens automatically, and the native's striving will be oriented toward maturing into an individual who is capable of making and carrying out independent decisions.

When a vertically aligned Moon-Node horoscope stands in contrast to a horizontally aligned radix, the position is reversed. Now the (possibly over-emphasized) individual "I"-standpoint needs toning down so that more attention can be paid to others. See Chart 16 on page 176 for an example placement. The native should be willing to enter into a binding agreement with one or more individuals from the working or family environment. In the following horoscope examples we can clearly see from the lie of the aspect picture that, in the Moon-Node horoscope, there is a strongly individual placement, and that, in the radix, the same aspects are aligned with the horizontal "I"-"You" plane. Here the stage of development mentioned above applies.

Displacement of Planets

In the house displacement we can study the individual planets. We observe the houses in the Moon-Node horoscope in which they stood, and the houses in the radix in which they stand now. One can ask oneself: "Shall I go along with this because it is my own development dynamics, or shall I resist it and decide I won't do it?" The major planets are particularly important in this connection because they are concerned with changes in the development of the personality. We shall consider this in more detail later.

If, in the Moon-Node horoscope, the Sun was on the Descendant for example and now, in the radix, stands on the Ascendant, the native needs to break free from "You"-dependency and to

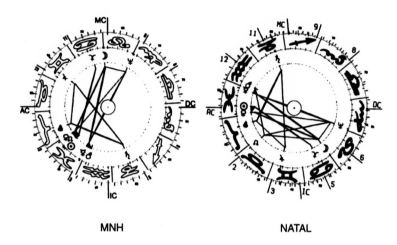

MNH   NATAL

Chart 16. Stephan. March 11, 1930, 7:00, Steffisburg, Switzerland, Koch houses. Birth data from birth certificate.

become an "I"-person. If the Sun falls from the upper sector to the lower, the native can no longer enjoy free expression of his or her individuality but must learn to move in the collective and to take his or her obligations and affiliations seriously.

It is quite obvious that a displacement from one side to the other is much harder to cope with than a shift from one house to the next. One may also consider that such a drastic movement from one pole to the other is impossible in a single life but requires several lives for its accomplishment. Therefore there is no need to despair if one is confronted with a great change in one's horoscope. But, in any case, displacements of the entire aspect picture from one side to the other rarely occur.

Displacement of Sun and Moon

In Chart 17 we can immediately see that, in the Moon-Node horoscope, the center of gravity of the aspect picture is with the Sun

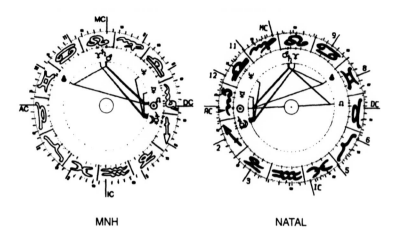

MNH   NATAL

Chart 17. Maria. November 14, 1947, 07:20, Winterthur, Switzerland. Koch houses. Birth data from birth certificate.

and Moon on the "You"-side; whereas, in the radix, it is on the "I"-side. Obviously, in former lives, Maria has experienced intense "You" relationships. The Sun at the "You"-point of the Moon-Node horoscope is always a sign that the native has been eager to do anything for a partnership. In several lives it was certainly the mainspring of her life to find a partner, to devote herself to others, and to set aside her own development. She has found security in the partnership, and has seen marriage as setting the social seal of approval on her own personality, and as the measure of her own competence (since Saturn is on the MC, this means her competence as a mother among other things). Certainly many lives have been devoted to this turning toward the "You" until Maria has undergone all possible experiences and has reached a degree of perfection in this regard.

People with the Sun in the 7th Moon-Node house have laid up a rich store of experience where partnership is concerned. They know all about love and marriage, fidelity, doing one's duty, responsibility, the spirit of sacrifice, and unselfishness. They are also aware of all the negative aspects of partnership: incompatibility, conflict, disputes, hatred, rejection, unkindness, grievances, separation, divorce, breaches of contact, egotistical motives, expediency, making sure that "I'm all right." This list could easily be extended. In any case, people with this Moon-Node house heavily tenanted can be called "7th-house specialists."

It is clear from the law of evolution that this development must be followed through to the end in order to give validity to the other side of the horoscope. Therefore, it comes as no surprise that everything is reversed in the radix. Maria's Sun is now at the "I"-point, the Ascendant. Naturally, this means that she ought to develop her personal ego and to break free from her "You"-dependency. Of course the old pull of the "You" will always be there, for the Moon-Node horoscope represents a long-lasting effect which is stored in the shadow.

With such a drastic displacement from one side of the chart to the other, development is likely to be hurried on by some profoundly disturbing experience. Only in this way can ingrained habits be overcome. The native is liable to suffer a trauma in early childhood. Here the experience was one that spoiled the sense of closeness to the "You."

Biographical Note

Maria was the first daughter after two ͜ʋas and, that being so, a great fuss was made of her—as is often made of children with the Sun on the AC. But she has a square to the Sun from a Mars-Saturn conjunction, and her birth was attended by a certain amount of stress. Her mother had had a stillbirth the previous year, and the parents were desperately hoping that Maria would be born safely. One can imagine their relief and joy when a healthy baby came into the world.

At age 5, which coincided with a transit over the Moon-Venus conjunction in the radix, Maria had a severe attack of nephritis and was hospitalized for three months. It was a painful experience for her to be left alone. She kept picturing how she had been left behind weeping on the stairs by her parents. She had to lie in bed in the isolation ward and had hardly any contact with other people. Thus, even as a small girl, she had been thrown back on herself. This trauma had initiated the required "I"-development. A fear of being left alone has haunted Maria throughout her life until now; and yet, in this very experience, lies the key to her further development or to some task later in life.

When Maria came for consultation, her Age Point was passing through Gemini—a good sign for improvement. She wants to be instructed in psychology and astrology so as to be able to help others to find the way and the strength to be alone. In doing so she can turn her own weakness into a strength, in accordance with the old adage: "Every cloud has a silver lining." Thus in each trauma there lies hidden a seed of development. The realization of this hidden meaning or inner mandate to go on to better things is one of the finest gifts of house comparison.

Planets in the Same House

If a planet, Jupiter for example, stands in the 9th house both in the Moon-Node horoscope and in the radix, no change occurs. It can unstintedly draw on its resources. Its energy is not diverted to some other house as usually happens but is channeled direct from the unconscious to the conscious. As a rule, what we are dealing with is a mature ability, even though it does not always express itself in this house without complications.

Three-dimensionality

When there is no change in the house placement, the interpretation is particularly telling if one makes use of the law of development of three-dimensionality. Here I will describe the most important criteria of the three stages:

1. The stage of material confinement, determination, Saturnian crystallization;

2. The stage of emotional polarity, emotional conflicts, Lunar practical experience;

3. The stage of mental freedom, intelligence and will, Solar self-determination.

From this vantage point, one can easily discover whether a person can already fully use a certain ability on all three planes or still has some lessons to learn. If he or she stands at the second stage and keeps running backward and forward there, it is still possible, apparently, to reach the third stage in this life. If the native is locked into materialism, then he or she must first aspire to the second stage.

We have repeatedly established that many with a planet that does not change house are convinced that there is a task for them to finish, but often they have the feeling, "I can't do more," or, "I'll never learn that." Others protest that they have already exploited the house concerned to such an extent that they have no idea what could be left for them to learn. And yet these people do develop further.

Then there are others again with a planet in the same house who, as far as the theme of the house is concerned, have the feeling that everyone is like themselves. They are amazed when they eventually discover that there are other ways of thinking and other types of character. For a long time they live under the delusion that while others may need to come to terms with this quality, they themselves do not. Since it has looked the same to them from time immemorial, they think that it must do so to everybody. Such a mistaken belief that we are all alike and see everything in the same way, is one possible effect of planets that remain in the same house.

Sun in the Same House

It seems best to explain this by means of an example. In Chart 18, shown below, the Moon-Node horoscope has the Sun in Gemini in the 8th house, and in the radix it is right on the cusp of the 8th house. Thus the theme of the 8th house is an "old theme" and Nora is already well acquainted with it.

In the first stage, everything to do with social structure, status, and social position stands in the forefront of the conscious mind. This person knows how to behave in any company, observes good form and etiquette, and is able to secure a place in society. The native knows all the tricks for getting on in life and can always discover a loophole in the law through which to wriggle out of awkward situations. With the Sun, we want to be accepted; to be someone who possesses a recognized position and has a reputation as a law-abiding citizen. Several lives have been spent learning everything to do with this area.

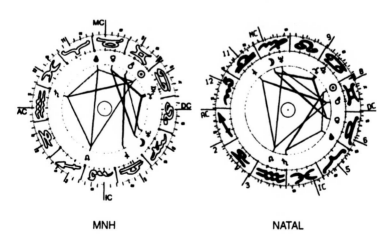

MNH   NATAL

Chart 18. Nora. June 19, 1934, 17:26, Budapest, Hungary. Koch houses. Birth data from birth certificate.

A Gemini Sun will "have its say" and is always eager to join in when external status is in question. The native has belonged to the propertied classes, has exercised power through money and real estate, also through public bodies and political parties (perhaps in the fields of police-work, taxation, civic administration, or some other form of officialdom), and has often been a judge. One can see, from the planetary stellium in the 8th house, the negative effects of this field—material losses, disinheritance, quarrels, corruption, bias, unscrupulous deals, making personal gain from other people's money, fortune-hunting, theft of goods or ideas. Many are subject to a dynastic compulsion which they have to subdue in order to be able to look after the affairs of others.

In the second stage, there is always a crisis, a transformation brought about by states of conflict. The 8th house contains the psychological and spiritual demands of the eternal "death-and-renewal" known as transformation. This speeds up development in such a way that the native experiences times of total reversal where everything that was important in the past suddenly loses its appeal. "Death-and-renewal" knows no half measures, but produces quakes in which structures that have served their purpose are totally demolished. The forces of change are brought to bear on the expansive solar ego, with continual urging to sacrifice all worldly attachments. During such a transformatory crisis, the above-mentioned titles, offices, and estates must be abandoned.

In certain situations we have the feeling that nobody takes a personal interest in us, that we have a function to fulfill and are nothing more than purveyors of materials, goods, finance, or intellectual currency. Inside, we feel unappreciated. The autonomy-seeking Sun rebels, wants to throw off the burden but is incapable of doing so, and keeps falling back into old routines. The transformation process of the 8th house and the permanent change in motivation holds the "I" in a vise-like grip. Even when it feels dependent and powerless, and the plaything of circumstances, of the world, of the paternal relationship, it must go through the narrow gate of change.

In the third stage, the urge toward another form of existence prevails. The native is no longer occupied only with material existence and its preservation, but turns toward the higher things in life. Just as the phoenix rises from the ashes to the celestial realms, so the purged solar ego turns to spiritual things. The individual dips into esotericism, and desires to study the background of life, death, and destiny. He or she takes an interest in the riddle set by the transience of earthly existence and the decay of physical forms when compared with the enduring quality of the soul. In the third stage of the 8th house, the transformed solar ego will definitely experience the uniqueness of the self, the immortality of the soul, and its attempt to be original in the established world. It will no longer crave for power and wealth.

When these bottled-up forces of the solar ego discharge themselves explosively and the soul emerges, the native crosses the threshold of initiation. In the highest stage, the 8th house is a door that opens onto the transcendental world and links us with dimensions of being pertaining to the other side. That is why this house used to be known as "the house of death." An interest in the frontiers of knowledge, in metaphysical contemplation, and in spiritual experiences, rises to such a pitch at this stage that all barriers can be surmounted. Nothing matters any more except spiritual growth. The enjoyment of a meaningful life is made possible by the perception that there are forms of existence beyond the threshold. The native makes contact with celestial beings, receives inner guidance, and is carried far beyond mundane matters.

Rules for Interpretation

Peregrine Planets in the MNH

On examining the Moon-Node horoscope, we may see planets that fall outside the aspect picture. They stand alone and are therefore separate. In the unconscious they feel like lost children, being parts or powers of the ego that are hardly accessible to everyday consciousness. Compulsions are usually caused by unaspected planets or by isolated aspects between two planets. We know from our rules of interpretation that even in the radix detached planets or aspect figures represent an "autonomous mechanism" in the conscious mind, a mechanism that for the most part works without our having any say in the matter. Many people blame its activities on their environment, partner, parents, brothers and sisters, or some other convenient scape-goat. (See Anna's chart, Chart 23 on page 213.)

Secondary Personalities

In psychosynthesis we speak of "secondary personalities." These are automatically functioning mechanisms of our psyche, composed invariably of a number of elements (planets, signs, houses, aspect structures). Therefore we cannot derive them from peregrine planets in the MNH. They come from all three horoscopes. With peregrine planets we must, above all, consult the house horoscope. If, for example, an unaspected planet receives supplementary aspects there, we can say that the native has further learned something essential. By taking advantage of what is offered by the environment, he or she can make this planet more and more meaningful in life.

If, on the other hand, a planet or a single aspect remains isolated in all three horoscopes, then we may be sure that we are dealing with a secondary personality—a fragment split off from the "I." Peregrine planets in all three horoscopes can gain full autonomy and are then experienced as independent, shifting or oscillating entities. The extreme case is schizophrenia, in which the entities or secondary personalities are strangers to one another. As long as they are conscious, they may be thought of as role-playing functions; employed (with a certain degree of awareness) as the situation may seem to demand. Whether the role is that of a housewife, a mother, or a supervisor, say, depends on the nature of the planets involved.

Oppositions

Special attention should be paid to the oppositions in the Moon-Node horoscope, because they have to do with old routines that keep being performed. In oppositions between two or more planets we have to allow for rigid structures that are not easily modified. The natives continually undergo the same experiences, make the same mistakes, and always react in the same old way. They find it very hard to change. In this connection, we need to observe whether or not the opposition lies along a different axis in the radix. If it does so, the programmed behavior switches to a different area of life and has to adapt to fresh circumstances, which probably comes hard. Especially in a T-square, the state of mind remains for a long time stubborn and unreasonable. Such people react in given situations just as the Moon-Node horoscope indicates. Recent research has shown that many people are still living in their Moon-Node horoscope and have not caught up with what their conscious ought to be doing now.

The Same Axis

It sometimes happens that an opposition remains on the same axis in both horoscopes, so that the same structure is active.One can say that it undergoes no change in this life, and the native can play his or her part unhampered by problems. But one can also say: "Wait a minute! I am wrapped up in a compulsive old routine which is absorbing all my energies." A character trait becomes a secondary personality, is always in the foreground as a strong influence and acts as the leader of the band throughout life. Everything depends on what planets form this opposition and on what axis it lies. On a cardinal axis (1/7 and 4/10) the will is much involved, there is a desire to attain goals, to cut out competitors, and to be first in rank and importance. On a fixed axis (2/8 and 5/11) an "old opposition" will immensely reinforce the inertia, one stands on one's rights, is inflexible in one's demands, and will not give ground by so much as a single inch. On a mutable axis (3/9 and 6/12) the theme of learning, of love, and of liberty, is squeezed into a rigid thought-form. One is quite happy to live without an objective, impulsively or in a chaos, and sees no reason to be self-disciplined or to consider the wishes or requirements of others.

Power Structures

Beginners in astrology are apt to start thinking of crime and punishment when a power structure is evident in the Moon-Node horoscope. This structure can be recognized either in an opposition on the 4/10 axis or when Pluto or the Sun are near the MC, or Capricorn and Cancer are heavily tenanted. Then it rather looks as if one has misused one's power in a former life, and it may be conjectured that one was a ruler or member of the nobility who treated the populace harshly.

It is interesting, however, that those who have a power structure in the Moon-Node horoscope are usually violently allergic to any exercise of power. They themselves will not possess power under any circumstances, and they turn against anyone who does possess it. As a compensation, they frequently have an authority problem and cannot subordinate themselves. If someone orders them around or treats them unfairly, they become annoyed, aggressive, or enraged. This is due to the reversal discussed in the previous chapter: the about-face through 180 degrees, which always causes a reflection in the Moon-Node horoscope. With such placements one can experience either the one or the other pole.

Moon-Node Age Point

As mentioned earlier, we also have an Age Point in the Moon-Node horoscope, and this shows us where we are in the horoscope at any given time. The Moon-Node Age Point traverses the twelve lunar houses in the usual seventy-two years. Just as a reminder, it is worth repeating that the MN-AP begins at the Ascending Node and travels clockwise (i.e., in the opposite sense to the normal Age Point) in six-year stages from one house to another. See figure 14 on page 188. Since the Moon-Node houses are all the same size (30 degrees), this works out at exactly five degrees for each year of life.

We can also read the corresponding dates direct from the Moon-Node Age Point printout from the API-Computer Cortex or from the aspect calculator.[1] But please note that the computer printout reverses the Moon-Node horoscope, i.,e., the zodiac signs are laid out clockwise so that we can number the houses from left to right as usual. With a little practice, we can immediately see where we are in the Moon's Node system at age 12, for example. We can then study the aspects and note whether or not we reacted to any of these. It has been found, over the years, that not everybody reacts to the usual MN-AP aspects. On the other hand, we observe that in crises of spiritual development the Moon-Node Age Point has more influence than that of the radix.[2]

Crossing-points C1 and C2

Another important element in interpretation is the crossing of the two Age Points. During a lifetime of seventy-two years, the two Age Points meet twice. We call these encounters "crossing-points." In the Age Progression computer printout these points are labeled C1 and C2. We have already gone into the interpretation of these points in the first part of the book.

Here we would like to suggest one easy way of locating the crossing-point: If there is a planet in the same house in the Moon-

---

[1]Interested readers can request these printouts from API(UK) Chart Data Service, or they can be generated by software programs generating Huber-style charts. See page x.
[2]See also "The Horoscope of Jiddhu Krishnamurti" in *Astrology and the Spiritual Path* (Samuel Weiser 1990), pp 123-138.

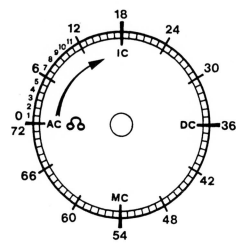

Figure 14. Moon's Node Age Point.

Node horoscope and the radix, then that is where the two Age
Points cross. Many students find the crossing-point simply by
beginning with a planet in the same house. Of course, the crossing-point can also occur in a house that is unoccupied. Then we
usually find the same sign there.

A planet at the crossing-point signifies a major turning point
in life. Generally such far-reaching changes take place slowly. They
are processes of transformation which commence two or three
years before the crossing-point and do not reach completion until
two through five years after transit.

In Chart 19 (page 189), Uranus stands in Cancer just after the
DC both in the radix and in the Moon-Node horoscope. The crisis of change began at the entry into Cancer and was at its height
when Uranus was transited. Various factors came together at this
stage of the Age-progression: 1) Change of sign; 2) Transit of the
DC; 3) Crossing of the two Age Points; 4) AP conjunction with

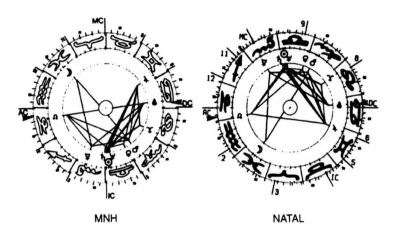

MNH   NATAL

Chart 19. Susanne. October 19, 1953, 13:45, Grindelwald, Switzerland. Koch houses. Birth data from birth certificate.

Uranus; and 5) The opposition of the Moon's Nodes in the Moon-Node horoscope. All these factors together produced a typical, basically Uranian, alteration in awareness. Life changed for the native on all planes simultaneously: family, partnership, self-image, goals, and understanding. She decided to study astrology, met new people, and started a new occupation.

The Crossing Axis

The two crossing-points are opposite one another and are defined according to the theme of the axis. If the "crossing axis" is in houses 1 and 7, as in the illustrative horoscope in Chart 19, the experience of the "I" and the "You," i.e., the human encounter and contact situation is a particularly important theme in the life. (Further details have been given in the chapter on basic themes of the life, in the first part of the book.)

Age Point Opposition

A further element of interpretation becomes available when the two Age Points oppose one another. This opposition occurs every thirty-six years and is square the crossing-points C1 and C2. If, for example, the crossing axis happens to lie in houses 3 and 9 of the radix (see figure 15, below), the Age Point opposition will take place on the 6/12 axis. It is plain, therefore, that in each case one of the three cross qualities (cardinal, fixed, mutable) is involved in the superordinate life theme.

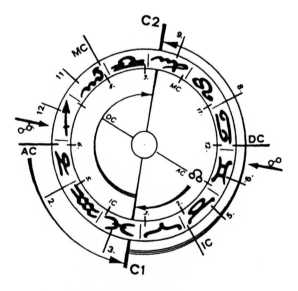

Figure 15. The crossing-point on the 3/9 axis.

Chapter 4

Personality Planets in the Moon-Node Horoscope

Introduction • Sun in the MNH • Displacement of Sun • Example
Horoscope: Social Worker • Moon in the MNH • Example
Horoscope: Nora • Displacement of Moon • Saturn in the
MNH • Example Horoscope: Hildegard • Displacement of
Saturn • Personality Planets in the Crosses in the MNH • Cardinal
Personality in the MNH • Fixed Personality in the MNH • Mutable
Personality in the MNH •

Introduction

I f it is true that development of self-awareness is the aim and purpose of our whole human evolution, then the manifestation of
the "I" and the unfolding of the personality on an ever higher
plane is very important. The task of each human being is to
become conscious of the self as an individual and to express this
self-awareness as fully as possible. All the experiences of life in the
course of one's development are useful for promoting individuation and have something to say to the ego. It is the office of the "I"
to collect and process these experiences. Without the central,
thinking, and intelligent self, no development is possible. The
conscious "I" is able to sort out, and objectify, what is experienced,
and to fit it into a wider scheme of relationships. When we take a
look at evolution and reincarnation, it is evident that the personality planets play a leading role in the interpretation.[1]

---

[1]This is discussed in greater detail in "Personality and Integration," the second part
of Bruno Huber's *Astrological Psychosynthesis*, published by The Aquarian Press, London, in 1991. An American edition of this book will be published by Samuel Weiser in 1995.

Saturn, the Moon, and the Sun (figure 16) are those points in the Moon-Node horoscope from which we can tell in what areas of life (house placements) and in what ways (signs) our "I" has already unfolded or developed self-awareness, and where we have acquired power, autonomy, and know-how. By comparing the situation in the Moon-Node horoscope with that in the radix, we discover in what other areas (houses) our "I" ought to be developing now. In fact there is a systematic dynamics of development which we should recognize and accept. From the Moon-Node house in which the Sun, the Moon, or Saturn is posited, the road to where this personality planet is domiciled in the radix can be short or long, easy or hard. A knowledge of the way forward and a determination to take it, contain immense possibilities for development of the personality.

Thus a careful study of these qualities and developmental tendencies as revealed in the two charts together, helps us to decide which changes, transformations, and new goals are required by our "I." Many people find it liberating to know the direction in which they should and must make further progress. Often, when guilt feelings are present, it is good to have this new sense of purpose that sets the energies flowing again. The "I" is strengthened by such knowledge and can release itself from any blockages that are holding up development. As others have discovered before us, being ourselves is much easier when we are sure we are on the right road. As long as we are in doubt, we are ill-prepared to meet

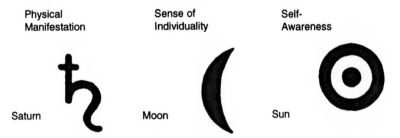

Physical Manifestation	Sense of Individuality	Self-Awareness
Saturn	Moon	Sun

Figure 16. Personality planets.

the contingencies of development; but when we deliberately walk this personal path, and when we flow with the stream of developmental dynamics, we are complying with the natural laws of life. These tell us unmistakably that we can never omit any phase of development, and should never rest on our laurels. Change is a constant necessity for us, for life is in perpetual motion. The wise thing to do is to keep on the move and willingly adjust to new conditions. And it is wiser still to discover from a comparison of the two charts the object of our development in this present life. In order to enable the reader to do so, we shall first point out the interpretative possibilities of the three personality planets (Sun, Moon, and Saturn) in the Moon-Node horoscope and then illustrate the potential for transformation contained in the displacement of these planets—which usually occurs, of course, when we switch from the MNH to the radix.

Sun in the MNH

The Sun in the Moon-Node horoscope indicates definite status, a degree of autonomy, and the exercise of power. In the house it occupies, self-awareness and a certain authority have been attained. The field has been won, and control has been established in this sphere of life. With the Sun, the native has been able to acquire the relevant capabilities, to set the tone, and to make independent decisions. He or she has obtained know-how in this area: a knowledge of what to do in order to act independently. Everything is done to bring the affairs of the house under the native's control. There is no reliance on others, and any interference on their part is vigorously resisted. Directives from outside are refused. Therefore (in accordance with the sign involved) the native has imposed his or her will on others, and involved (or even exploited) them in seeking his or her own goals. Nearly always, with the Sun, there is this ability to function autonomously, to work at something permitting self-expression, to achieve status, and to influence others.

The placement of the Sun is also an indication of the power struggles in this field. Probably we have had to do battle with rivals, to contend with adversaries, dissidents, interlopers, robbers, and enemy leaders, and to defend our own territory. Certainly, with the influx of solar energy, our will-power and fighting strength are increased, we make our presence felt, square up to people and are not easily brushed aside. Finally, the Sun is our core of personal vitality and indicates our legitimate claim on life. Its aspects show whether or not we have used the right means to fight for our sphere of influence. As already said, our shadow has two sides. With the Sun we have doubtless exercised power, and have certainly at one time or another been deprived of power and toppled from our "throne," perhaps even killed by a foreign army. Human history is full of rises and falls. We have been present at the collapse of power blocs and civilizations, and have seen wars and upsets of all kinds.

Displacement of Sun

The development and transformation of self-awareness is discernible in the displacement from one house to another. As described in the previous chapter, normally the position of the Sun switches from some house in the MNH to another house in the radix. If a 2nd house MNH-Sun is found in the 3rd house of the radix, nothing very drastic has happened. One merely has to develop into the next house—something that is managed usually without much difficulty. A change from the 12th to the 5th house, on the other hand, would be quite a leap; because the shift is from the "I"-side to the "You"-side, and from a house with a theme of isolation and retirement to a house calling for one's self-awareness to be tested in practice. Obviously, this step is not so easy to take and requires much more time. How the displacement will work out in practice always depends on the case history of the individual concerned. For the elucidation of this point, we invite the reader to examine the charts below:

In Chart 20 (below), we see the Sun on the cusp of the 3rd house in the MNH, and on the cusp of the 6th house in the radix. Thus the displacement is from one mutable house to the next mutable house. There is no great alteration in the theme of the crosses. Therefore only the house itself and its theme matter here.

This lady comes from a family traditionally associated with teaching. Her father was a teacher, her grandfather was a teacher, and her two sisters also entered the profession. The 3rd-house Sun in the MNH in Gemini is a first-class placement for educational work. Very probably, she has already undertaken such work in a former life. Throughout her childhood it was assumed that she, too, would become a teacher. Her father (the Sun) was continually making this suggestion. However, she decided not to follow her father, because she wanted to break out of this mold, and she chose to enter the social services. The Sun on the 6th cusp of the radix is a fine placement for this.

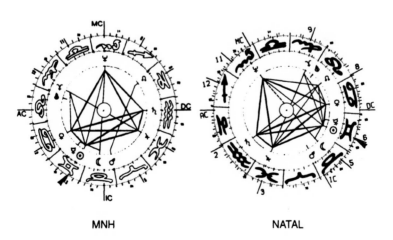

MNH   NATAL

Chart 20. Social Worker. May 31, 1962, 21:55. Zurich, Switzerland. Koch houses. Birth data from birth certificate.

With the Moon's Node transit at age 23, she made up her mind to train as a social worker. She took this step entirely on her own initiative, and had to secure the necessary tuition without her father's help. With the entry into Gemini, the sign in which her Sun stands on the 6th cusp in the radix, she took up a new post as a social worker, and found it very fulfilling. Here we discover that the Sun in the Moon-Node horoscope often denotes a family tradition, as if the shadow were trying to manifest through the family.

Moon in the MNH

The placement of the Moon in the Moon-Node horoscope shows where we have fully developed our emotions: our feelings of sympathy and antipathy, joy and grief, excitement and confidence. Many times, in the house where the Moon is domiciled, we have been able to remain a child, we have been cared for, others have taken the responsibility, and have tended and cherished—if not pampered—us. In this house position in the Moon-Node horoscope, we see areas of life we abandoned to others, areas where we made ourselves dependent and are still in our minority. It is a house position containing such a mixture of fear and irresponsibility that we are incapable of looking after ourselves.

The placement of the Moon also gives an indication of love affairs. Here one experiences on all sides happiness and sorrow, worth-while relationships, emotional dependency, lost love, etc. The native has learned to function in contacts along the lines laid down in the house position of the Moon in the MNH. Certain behavior patterns are repeated today although, by rights, they belong to the past.

All experiences that are polar in character are stored in the Moon: both those we have enjoyed and those that have brought suffering. Our emotional nature retains its links with the past in a way that is indicated by the Moon's placement in house and sign. We are haunted by hopes and wishes of long ago. Often we dream of having a secure relationship with people with whom, in a previous existence, we were deeply in love. We want to return to them and grieve that they are no more with us; and we feel forsaken and misunderstood. Many times we are gripped by a tormenting fear that we shall never be loved as greatly as we were in former lives. Continually, from the depths of our being, there rises a pining for this secure relationship with people who care for us, side with us, and keep us from harm. Frequently we imagine that such relationships will necessarily recur, and have to learn by taking some hard knocks in love that this is not so, and that we must proceed with our development even when it hurts.

Displacement of Moon

With a displacement of the Moon to an entirely different house, we recognize that "the wind is blowing from another quarter," the old days are gone and we have to develop our emotions and contacts in a new direction. In Chart 21 (below), we observe a dis-

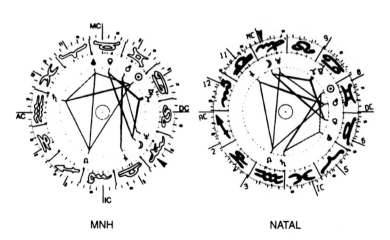

MNH   NATAL

Chart 21. Nora. June 19, 1934, 17:26. Budapest, Hungary. Koch houses. Birth data from birth certificate.

placement of the Moon from the 5th house in the MNH to the MC
in the radix. Here a relatively big step from below to above needs
to be taken in the development.

The Moon in the 5th house is always a sign of childlikeness.
It can make one a child who is not worried overmuch about 5th-
house matters. Love, eroticism, having children, artistic expression, the spirit of adventure and risk-taking, but also a lack of
sophistication, naïveté, credulity, devotion, purity, and harmless-
ness, are qualities of the Moon in this house in Virgo. The 5th
house could be called a "cosmic game," where we are protected
and are able to be children. Certainly, Nora must have had
opportunities in former lives to enjoy, light-heartedly, what this
house has to offer. She was satisfied on all sides with love and protection. Now the Moon makes a talent-triangle with Venus and
the conjunction of Mercury and Pluto. This cheerful unconcern
is undoubtedly a talent or inner gift, helping her not to take too
gloomy a view of things. In her unconscious is an emotional
structure that gives her an easy way with others, and even children (represented by the 5th house) are important emotional
partners.

The displacement in the present life is to the MC, the individuation point in the horoscope, where one is conspicuous to
everybody and desires to be self-sufficient. This ascent to individuation of the emotional body is a big step. The native must now
take her own development seriously, and must work on herself
with the object of further improvement, so that she can realize her
professional aims (10th house). Clearly, with the Moon in Virgo, a
helping profession is indicated, which here is an inner calling.
The special quality of Nora's feelings is practically her leading
characteristic, and people can detect this lunar quality in her. She
does everything with devotion and conscientiousness, and tries to
perform her tasks to a high standard.

As a matter of fact, she trained in alternative medicine and
then turned her back on her social position in order to go out
and serve others. Our example in the last chapter had a similar
placement of the Sun and was also of someone in a helping pro-

fession. Here we recognize that further development is necessary on the emotional plane—from the irresponsible infantile emotional "I" into a fully aware person with a career of serving others and able to impart to them something of her spiritual purity and innocence.

Saturn in the MNH

Saturn, the physical pole of the "I," is connected with the ability to anchor oneself successfully in bodily existence. As the planet of form and demarcation, it creates shapes and structures that endure. In the Moon-Node horoscope, Saturn is also the "dweller of the threshold," and symbolizes our material worries, our confinement to physical life. It is the unavoidable burden of all the tasks left over from former lives and of our striving for security and power. In addition to the instinct for self-preservation, Saturn represents the collective behavior deposited in us by various cultures—often to the detriment of our further progress.

Its effect in the Moon-Node horoscope could be described like this: we created a sphere of influence in line with the lunar house in which Saturn is posited, and nothing would prevail on us to relinquish it. We were specialists in this sphere, and by our skill we have ruled the roost and exercised power. Usually, it was through our strength of character that we managed to distinguish ourselves and command respect, thus gaining the authority and influence we needed to feel safe. In the house concerned we have reached a sheltered position, performed a respected function, and aspired to a station that gave us prestige and security. We had adherents as long as we were competent; but if we lost our competence they deserted us. Saturn always contains the experience of having had our day, of being old, worn out, and of no more use, or of being rejected. These contingencies are present as subliminal fears in this Moon-Node house.

Usually the exercise of power is not the same in Saturn as it is in the Sun. In Saturn it is the means, the functions, the formal authority, that secure for us certain privileges, power and influence. Saturnian power owes its existence to forms, functions and professional status. Many have gained and exercised authority in the Church or a government department. In the name of the Church or of the civil rulers, they have been able to issue orders, write directives that had to be obeyed, and not least inflict punishments. For example, a prison governor or an army officer does not exercise power of the Sun's type, but exercises power of Saturn's type. He or she has the backing of the law, which silences all opposition. Saturn operates with guilt feelings; others are reproved and put in their place, and conditions and prohibitions are laid down with fixed penalties for their infringement.

Saturn in a Moon-Node house represents, in the matters of that house, an uncompromising position. The native has consistently obeyed the rules, accepted restrictions, made sacrifices, and done everything to keep the law. He or she has followed the dictates of a church or government, with Spartan resolve has refused to give way to temptation, and has often behaved like a prisoner because unwilling or unable to have fun. Amusements were rejected as wicked, and much that would have made life easier was foregone. The native judged and criticized others who skipped along and did not treat things too seriously. Even in this present life, it still irritates him or her when people take lighthearted liberties. As mentioned already, in Saturn the structures are hardened and they persist through many incarnations. According to sign and aspect, they offer dogged resistance to the least change. Quite often we can diagnose an ossification of the ego, a refusal to develop further, a clinging to old structures. In this area of life, we often, indeed very often, react as if we were still an authority on it.

On turning to the radix, we shall probably find that Saturn is now in another house. This represents a new area of life in which it is necessary to learn lessons, to carry out our tasks and responsibilities, and to rethink our claims to authority. It is good if we cooperate deliberately in doing these duties. In any case, we should note that in the radix we exhibit inner strength and stability, independence and self-reliance. Certainly Saturn has a mission of bringing us to maturity to fulfill, therefore it is relatively easy to gain this inner strength if we choose to do so.

Displacement of Saturn

In the MNH for Hildegard, Saturn is on the cusp of the 11th house. See Chart 22 below. Planets in the 11th house of the Moon-Node horoscope point nearly always to membership in former lives of an elite social class, and usually to an aristocratic background—but also to dogmatic thinking of a formal religious character. The 11th house symbolizes, in addition to friends and elite groups, spiritual principles. Hildegard certainly lived uncompromisingly along these lines, renounced pleasures and entertainments, and made sacrifices in order to look good and noble.

Clerical status is the reincarnation archetype of Saturn in the 11th Moon-Node house. The native was a church leader, a bishop or an abbot, held sway over others, and could prescribe what must and

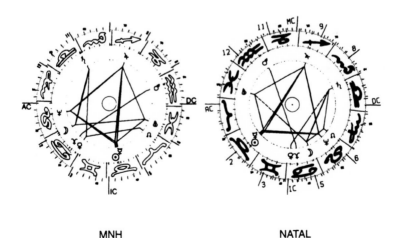

MNH   NATAL

Chart 22. Hildegard. May 10, 1924, 3:15, Bamberg, Germany. Koch houses. Birth data from birth certificate.

what must not be done. For example this is a typical placement for a mother superior who could freely discipline her nuns when they sinned or broke the rules. The authoritarian tendency to take advantage of her position to play the part of a stern judge is a well-defined unconscious pattern of behavior in Hildegard.

In the radix, Saturn has moved to the Low Point of the 7th house. A displacement from the cusp to the Low Point clearly signals a loss of power. In the house of partnership, the Low Point is experienced as a permanent deprivation of the right to rule. In the same measure that one was able, on the 11th cusp, to lay down the law to others, one is now under the control of the partner. In fact, in this life Hildegard has married a man who absolutely refuses to do anything she asks. She feels like a "voice crying in the wilderness," her years of effort have been fruitless. She has to learn something entirely new, and Saturn keeps facing her with fresh tasks. Such a placement now demands the development of a knowledge of human nature, which means that she must enter the "You"-space in order to serve the genuine needs of the "You" and give up her own pet ideas. She may no longer insist that she always knows best and is entitled to get her own way, but must understand that each person has an inner truth and a conscience which she must learn to respect.

Personality Planets in the Crosses in the MNH

The illustrated "displacements" of the three personality planets have shown how interpretations might be made in practice. Obviously, the basic variations for all Moon-Node houses and planetary occupations of signs have been interpreted and evaluated according to the Huber Method.

In order to make the task of interpretation easier, we shall now explain how the three Crosses in the MNH are specific motivations of the personality planets. The descriptions and the guides to interpretation supplied here contain an essential key for the correct apprehension and understanding of the developmental dynamics involved in a shift from the Moon-Node horoscope to the radix. These descriptions are valid for the houses and, to a lesser extent for the signs, too. In addition, each interpreter can take for granted the previously described characteristics of the Sun, the Moon, and Saturn.

Cardinal Personality in the MNH

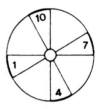

People with the Sun, Moon, or Saturn in the cardinal houses 1, 4, 7, and 10, have nearly always attained a successful expression of their identity in these areas of life. In the area of life corresponding to the house placement, they were able to do or not do whatever they liked. They learned the exercise of power and tried to come out on top in every situation. A striving for dominance, career-mindedness, hierarchic systems of rank, improved performance, and competitive behavior, are merely a few of the possible characteristics of this cross. Also there are invariably claims to originality and uniqueness sometimes used to out-do others. These people were respected, feared, admired, or else attacked. Rivalries usually occur on this cross, and we must be prepared to meet them.

This is the cross of will and might. With personality planets one is able to defend one's position by every possible means. One learned in former lives how to eliminate others and to seize control. In no circumstances did one tolerate interference or rivalry. One felt compelled to be the moving spirit behind everything, was able to be autonomous, and always desired to be the first and the best. Several lives have been spent in extending, defending and retaining influence and power in this house. Nevertheless, defeats must also have occurred from time to time. As already said, everything is two-edged in the MNH; certainly one has had to get to know the reverse side of the coin—for defeats spell development in the cardinal cross.

Fixed Personality in the MNH

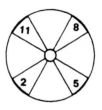

The Fixed Cross is the cross of perseverance. Personality planets in a fixed house (2, 5, 8, 11) in the MNH are adept at acquiring, retaining, collecting, and preserving things, in the area of life concerned. Because all processes in the fixed cross are quantitative, there is often repeated confinement to material things, possessiveness of people or positions, claims to power through one's position, beliefs, or connections, etc. Owing to the desire for repetition inherent in this house, the personality planets reveal deeply entrenched patterns of behavior in the psyche. These continue to work subliminally in this life, even if the planets now occupy cardinal or mutable houses. Many suffer from an inner urge to monopolize and hold on to everything, to accumulate possessions, to own others and to keep them tied down, in order to enhance self-worth.

In all the fixed houses there is a definite security motif, and it produces automatic reactions in this life. Whenever these people find themselves in what looks like a hopeless situation, they nearly always escape from it scot free somehow or other. It seems that their personality planets in the MNH operate as an automatic safety device. They possess an unconscious know-how or instinct to prevent losses and to avoid dangers, especially those that could affect their personal comfort, convenience, property, preserves, substance, status, etc.

And yet loss is the development factor of the fixed cross. The dread of losing something and the refusal to give up something can directly help to bring about what is feared most. Separations and losses must be accepted if one wants to develop further.

Mutable Personality in the MNH

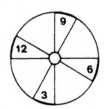

The Mutable Cross is the cross of human relationships, and of conformity, contact, and love. Here the individual desires to be loved for himself or herself. Everything is done to make oneself attractive, and to become the recipient of the esteem and popularity that will increase the sense of identity. One is very much aware that love is the most beautiful gift in life. All will be sacrificed for love, because love is the hope of the world. One aims to be pleasant, sensitive, well-educated, and well-bred—to look good in the eyes of others.

In the mutable cross, we have an aptitude for helping people; we take an interest in them, and do what we can for their welfare. However, this benevolence always implies that we want to make ourselves loved: a covert egoism lurks behind it. In the mutable houses (and signs), the "I" is individualistic, and will act voluntarily without making a firm commitment or allowing itself to be pressured. But because it cannot make a clear and unequivocal stand, it is liable to be influenced after all. We may well become a plaything of the world around if the principle of adaptability is overdone.

Religion, philosophy, ethics, civilized values, art, and literature, have to do with the mutable cross, and therefore with the personality. Many natives were formerly under the influence of a strong mind, a dogma, an ecclesiastical authority, or an institution. They clung to a stable pattern of thought, with which they were able to hold their wavering in check. They would not admit they had willingly surrendered their freedom, but felt that they had been deceived, betrayed, and exploited. For this reason, many now emphatically refuse to obey orders. Because of the demand for freedom inherent in mutability, they will not under any circumstances have someone in charge of them again.

And yet, the mutable cross lives mostly at the expense of the two other crosses; but natives may not acknowledge this and will not pay the price, imagining that to live intensely is to do their share. Often these people will have had problems with being dependent. A sense of powerlessness, illnesses, hindrances, jails, and hospitals, as well as voluntary renunciation of material wealth in cloisters, also belong to this cross. Many times, the cultivation of a religious, unworldly frame of mind has seemed promising to the "I" that wanted to develop. It seemed a way to make sense of life.

Chapter 5

Consultation Work Using Three Horoscopes

Fundamentals • Consultation Using the Moon-Node Horoscope •
Inspiring Trust • Effectiveness • Consultation Using Three
Horoscopes • The Story of the Discovery • Case 1: Neurosis
Linked with a Love Affair • Case 2: Emaciation as a Symptom
of a Mental Crisis • Concluding Thoughts •

Fundamentals

The way astrology is used has changed a great deal over the centuries. Today, many people look to astrology to supply answers to the deeper questions of life. They have become more interested in the idea of reincarnation; they want to penetrate the meaning and purpose of their lives, to know their karma, and to learn something about their true vocation. They would like to know why certain constellations or childhood traumas create so much trouble. Others would like to advance spiritually and are trying to rid themselves of false ideas and patterns of behavior. What is more, counselors, psychologists, educators, and physicians are looking for new and improved methods of understanding human psychology and of dealing effectively with those who come to them for help. Many of these experts are taking a fresh look at astrology and are successfully using it as a diagnostic tool in their practice. Now, in the Moon-Node horoscope, they have an additional resource which throws light on the background of human fate and on the causes of deep-seated problems. Astrologers and psychologists should pay increased attention to the Moon-Node horoscope in consultation work: then they will be able to see the deeper connections.

During a consultation, it is the following situations, more than any, that lead us to turn to the Moon-Node horoscope:

1) When a client who knows something of reincarnation seeks deeper answers to the problems of life;

2) In cases where the radix does not offer a satisfactory clarification of mental or spiritual problems;

3) When we suspect that the problem is a karmic one rooted in the shadow or in former lives;

4) When the individual wants to develop further, or wants to make sense of his or her life, or wants to trace fate through various incarnations.

Consultation Using the Moon-Node Horoscope

When interpreting the Moon-Node horoscope, we should make up our minds to adopt a positive attitude toward the client. The interpretation will not work without a humane and ethical approach. Giving advice on the basis of the Moon-Node horoscope requires more attentiveness, sensitivity, and awareness of our responsibility, not to mention experience, than does the interpretation of the natal chart. It requires us to distance ourselves internally from our own person, from our own inclinations and value judgments. It also requires us to possess a high degree of impartiality and integrity. The inner potential of the client should be discovered with interest and anticipation, but also we should try to locate the client's wrong attitudes and problems. The client should be treated seriously as a partner, and the horoscope should be studied and interpreted jointly with him or her. We must always be conscious of the responsibility that is ours when offering advice on the basis of the Moon-Node horoscope, because we are providing an extended voyage of self-discovery, a novel and fascinating chance for the native to discover his or her inner life. Since the depths we are helping the native explore are so intimate, it is, of course, extremely important to treat the client with respect.

Inspiring Trust

In this, as in any other consultation, the proceedings should be conducted in an atmosphere of trust. Only so can we gain entry to the shadow personality and initiate in the client a process of becoming conscious. We are dealing with deeply hidden parts of the being, to which any approach must be made with great care, because these parts shrink back from rough handling. Many repression mechanisms have been built around the shadow, shielding it and keeping it in darkness.

When working with clients, we must remember that the things we are trying to lay bare are covered by a "massive lid" which may seem to be made of concrete. Any tactless word, any clumsy or agitated movement on our part, can cause the lid to drop just as we are in the act of raising it. Therefore we need to cultivate an inner tranquility, and behave in a way that is friendly and not judgmental.

In no circumstances should we make a moralistic assessment or condemn clients. In evaluating karmic components we have to allow for the fact that by-gone civilizations had their own value-systems, from which it is hard for individuals to extricate themselves. Each karmic component has been woven into the collective fate of the society into which they have been born. Therefore it is inadmissible to utter a horrified exclamation at an "inquisition aspect," for example, or to speak of a guilt complex when we come across a judge archetype. It is not for us to apportion blame and to pass judgment. Nevertheless, what often happens is that clients are relieved straight away by the disclosure of hidden causes, and have a sense of being liberated from guilt. This can only happen if they are understood, not judged. Our attitude must be neither over-familiar nor distant, neither know-it-all nor indecisive; but between clients and ourselves there must exist a basis of trust, a complete openness and honesty. The best thing to do is to meditate briefly on the soul of the other person before each consultation.

Effectiveness

Some people who seek advice respond more immediately during a consultation to the explanation of their Moon-Node horoscope than they do to an interpretation of the radix. We could say that they live more in their shadow than they do in the present. At first, we assumed that this would be true mainly of young people, because their karmic past is not so far back, but we then discovered that the shadow motif is also fully present in the elderly.

Unfortunately, there are no rules for determining whether the shadow (and with it the Moon-Node horoscope) is totally or only partially repressed. We have had the opportunity to observe that people undergoing psychoanalysis, who had therefore already occupied themselves with the contents of their unconscious, responded much more quickly to the Moon-Node horoscope than did others who, until they came for advice, had never heard of such a thing. Apparently, what matters here is the measure of awareness and stage of development of the person concerned; perhaps also the evolutionary objective of that person's soul in its present life.

Consultation Using Three Horoscopes

The value of consultations using three horoscopes will become increasingly obvious as time goes by: primarily because one arrives quickly and efficiently at correct depth-psychological insights by comparing the House and Moon-Node horoscopes with the natal chart; but also because, by making this comparative study, it is possible to understand the whole individual on all three planes of his or her being. The client usually wants an investigation of his or her deepest layers, and a mere character analysis is not enough.

As we have said, a consultation of this sort must address the questions: "Who am I—From where have I come—Where am I going?" Life can be seen as a path of development, as a learning process; so that what happens to a person has a deeper meaning than appears on the surface. Unbearable life situations become bearable when viewed as necessary stages in a process of development extending over several incarnations.

In practice, what happens is this: if no further progress can be made with the radix, one can have recourse to the House horoscope or the Moon-Node horoscope for purposes of comparison. In any consultation over problems, a point is always reached where it is appropriate to look at the Moon-Node horoscope to discover the deeper meaning of the situation. When seen as part of a chain of cause and effect, problems often become less painful and are no longer blown up out of all proportion. The client can cope with them more easily, on the one hand through knowing why a life situation is as it is and not otherwise, and on the other hand by being able to identify them as their meaning becomes clear. In this way, many stressful experiences lose their sting, and in fact become assets on account of being necessary stages in the course of development.

In the above sense, a consultation using three horoscopes is a superb instrument for probing the inner depths of one's nature. When used responsibly, it quickly leads to far-reaching insights into one's life and being. Such knowledge can be life-changing.

The Story of the Discovery

The story of the discovery will be found informative by all who wish to employ the three horoscopes. In our work at the Arkan-

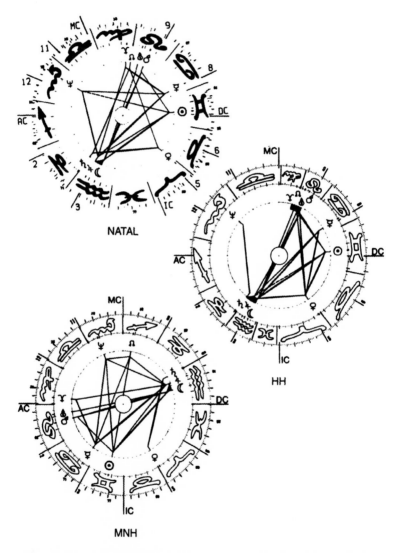

Chart 23. Anna. June 3, 1961, 19:50, Lucerne, Switzerland. Koch houses.
Birth data from birth certificate.

schule in Geneva, we scoured *Esoteric Astrology* by Alice Bailey for any suggestions that might stimulate and enrich our own research, and found one which we now recognize as an important key. We still have a vivid recollection of the following statement: in the long run, for a devotee of the new age, three horoscopes must be erected and superimposed.

One horoscope is organized around the Sun, one around the AC and one around the Moon. For a year we scratched our heads over this, and tried to figure out what it might mean. By 1958 we were still not getting anywhere. As we were then working in Florence with Roberto Assagioli at the Institute of Psychosynthesis, we put the problem at the back of our minds. Bruno Huber, while in Italy, was able to pursue his fundamental research in astrological psychology, and in 1964 we returned to Switzerland and founded the Astrologisch-Psychologische Institut in Adliswil near Zürich.

In the course of our teaching and consultancy work, Bruno Huber in collaboration with our son Michael, discovered (among many other innovations) the house horoscope, and shortly afterward the Moon-Node horoscope. For nearly eight years we worked in our consultancy with the three horoscopes, when in 1988 it suddenly struck us that these were what Alice Bailey must have meant. The radix is organized around the Sun, the House horoscope around the AC, and the Moon-Node horoscope around the Moon. Her encoded message seems strange at first, but it is nevertheless very striking and instructive, and it convinced us that we are on the right track.

We shall now endeavor to demonstrate this method by means of two illustrative cases.

Case 1: Neurosis Linked with a Love Affair

The individual in this example came for counselling in 1986 when she was nearly 25 years old. See Chart 23, on page 212. Her problem was a love affair leading to a neurotic crisis. She knew something about astrology and thought that because her partner had the Sun in Virgo, the sign occupied by her own Ascending Node, that this relationship might be karmic. She had heard that a Moon-Node connection could point to a so-called "old association," especially when it "clicks into place" in the house system with one of the partner's planets. "Clicking into place" is a term we use, in partnership analysis, for the situation where planets occupy the same place in a house in the two charts. Thus in this sense they are conjunct. Also the same sign position indicates a kindred quality, but usually not a relationship that will be formed in everyday life.

The fact is that Moon-Node relationships—even if they denote great intimacy—nearly always have to do with a significant learning process in a partnership. On the one hand there is an opportunity to come to terms with shared karma and, on the other hand, there is an acceleration of personal development due to the mutual knowledge and understanding enjoyed in a deep union. In some phases of the relationship, the learning processes have a radical and often unmanageable effect. Above all, if repressed wishes in the unconscious shadow region are sought out and activated, they can upset the even tenor of life. Nevertheless they do speed up development.

The Moon-Node horoscope before us now is an interesting case in point. Even at first sight, one cannot help noticing the isolated opposition between Saturn and Venus, which points to a problem with the mother and with the native's own femininity. The counseling as a whole turns on bringing into awareness the associated guilt feelings. And so, with such a deep-seated problem area, all three horoscopes should be consulted.

In making an assessment, we pay attention to the three planes, by inquiring after the "Where, How, and What." We ask, "Where is this problem rooted?" (MNH), "How does it manifest itself in the present situation?" (radix), "What contributions have been made by the actual life situation, i.e., what solutions has the milieu proposed during the upbringing?" (HH).

In Anna's Moon-Node horoscope the square between Venus (on the cusp of the 5th house) and Saturn (on the cusp of the 8th house) implies guilt feelings in the erotic sphere. Saturn in the

8th house, representing the establishment, suggests a condemnation of Venusian needs. Possibly, Anna was penalized in former lives for wanting to express her womanhood. She may even have been misused on account of love, with the result that she is unable to handle her femininity correctly. Her image of womanhood has been destroyed. Since the square is isolated, it cannot be controlled by the conscious. It has become a detached part in the shadow, a secondary personality.

Any isolated figure in the MNH has to do with contents that are extremely hard to integrate. Often there are complex compulsion mechanisms to which the native can be subject—especially when the Age Point activates them. Saturn imposes restraints that are so powerful that false reactions arise out of the unconscious, and the native may engage in self-punishment, or suffer from guilt feelings, or other neurotic conditions. The individual experiences anguish of soul: the outer reality may be quite harmless, but inside she feels she is horrible. With such a guilt complex, what matters is to lift it out of the unconscious, to look at it, to examine it intelligently, and to get it into proportion, so that it no longer causes distress. The radix can give a certain amount of help. In this case, the position of the Node in the radical 9th house points to a possible solution. We shall examine this in detail later.

In the radix we observe that the same square is incorporated in a trine. The Ascending Node (9th house) widens the problem and stimulates personal growth in the triangle of learning. Frequently, the conflict that causes so much trouble is the mainspring of further development. In the radix, Saturn occupies the 2nd house, the area to do with personal finance and feelings of self-worth. Thus Saturn is displaced from the MNH 8th house to the radical 2nd, implying a switch from subservience to self-determination, from the "You"-side to the "I"-side of the chart. It follows that, in this life, Anna ought to develop self-reliance and to disregard the opinions of the outside world. Venus remains in the 5th house, and does not alter her position. This factor turned out to

be significant, because when Venus was transited, Anna had a neurotic crisis.

In the House Horoscope we notice that instead of making a
square to Venus, Saturn now makes one to Neptune. The conflict
has been changed by the upbringing, and by the influence of the
milieu. Instead of Venus, which represents the female libido, we
have Neptune as the guiding image of the highest ideal of love,
which has to give consolation in the unsatisfying situation. When
she is in trouble, Anna is inclined to take refuge in a fantasy world.
In the HH, Neptune stands in the 11th house, where it juts out of
the aspect picture. It has a one-way aspect, reminiscent of a dead-
end-street. Fantasizing and building castles in the air are not the
answer. With this placement of Neptune in the HH, Anna projects
wishful thinking and delusive ideals onto her friendships and relationships, to the extent that Scorpionic sexual desire is stirred up.
She becomes entangled in internal contradictions and chases
phantoms, until her beautiful visions burst like bubbles.

The Venus Problem

It is advisable to let the client describe the problem; it then
becomes relatively easy to find confirmation or explanation in the
horoscope. Anna came for consultation shortly after her Age
Point had transited Venus. Both in the radix and in the Moon-
Node horoscope this planet stands near the cusp of the 5th house.
Whenever a planet has the same house position in both charts,
then—as we have already said—it does not undergo any change.
This almost always indicates that an old problem lies near the surface; not slumbering deep in the unconscious but, so to speak, just
under the skin. It no longer takes much effort to raise the problem into consciousness. But indicated, too, is the fact that some
past difficulty has still not been overcome and that the native is
once more confronted with this same old problem and has another opportunity to get the better of it. When Anna consulted us she
was suffering from restlessness, a sense of futility, and frustration.

So it is not surprising that, at that very time, the crossing of the two Age Points coincided with the transit of Venus. This hinted plainly enough at a decisive turning point in life.

The Case History

At age 24 (cusp 5) Anna attended an adult education school and became infatuated with her art teacher. She began to paint with abandon in order to please him. All her feelings were invested in this association. If he turned toward her, her heart thumped; she was head over heels in love and waited for some sign that he reciprocated her feelings. The slightest suggestion of this awakened in her the hope of fulfillment. She did all she could to attract the man's attention and then interpreted his response as evidence of his love. She doggedly nourished this hope until she was convinced that he loved her but was somehow unable to show that he did. At night, she dreamed of him, tossed from side to side in bed, and suffered mental anguish. She slid further and further into a state of neurosis associated with hallucinations.

The "Lapse"

One month later, exactly at the transit of Venus by the Age Point, matters went from bad to worse. She met an older man and rushed madly into a brief sexual adventure. Although she stopped the affair (she herself called it "debauchery" whenever she spoke of it) she persuaded herself that her heaven-sent beloved, the teacher, would spurn her because of this lapse. She suffered from strong guilt feelings, and when he actually found himself a girl-friend she was convinced that he had done it to punish her. She was in despair, and shed many tears. She could no longer remain at the school, but had to say she was ill, in order not to lose face entirely.

It is clear from the Moon-Node horoscope that what we have here is an "old propensity" for going astray. She certainly believed in former lives that the conjugal act was an obligation that she owed to her partner. In the MNH, she has the Moon conjunct Jupiter in the 7th house, which imparts to her "You"-dependence a philosophical and (because of the involvement of Aquarius) an ethical slant. Depending on the state of her psyche, her "old propensity" can be reactivated by Age Point aspects to repressed morbid factors and can produce compulsive behavior. In this case, the "emergence from the region of the shadow" took place with the Venus transit and the concurrent crossing of the two Age Points. This was too much all at once, and so she suffered from a nervous breakdown.

As far as her development was concerned, this was a good opportunity for Anna to come to grips with this old problem and to work on it voluntarily. She, herself, felt quite strongly that a past quality was affecting her from the shadow region. She was under an inner compulsion to do what she did, and said that she could not help herself. In respect of becoming aware, this must be treated as positive, because the contents of former lives were not brought to the surface by the manipulative methods of reincarnation therapy, but were experienced as a "normal activation" of the Age Point. Therefore she was able to come to terms with what happened and could even use it for her spiritual advancement.

The Consultation

In the consultation, we discussed the whole theme very thoroughly. I tried to point out the astrological reasons for her problem, and, among other things, explained to her the compensation mechanism, which Neptune in the House Horoscope provided as a way of escape from her erotic feelings. We talked about the red one-way aspect of Saturn in the HH. This impinges on the 11th house, in which one can so easily fall prey to deceptive ideal images. It was obvious that she was running after a captivating illusion. The problem was to find some way of making her see this in her current frame of mind. She could not tell if the teacher loved her; and I noticed that, when I wondered whether she might be deceiving herself, her voice trembled. She could not bear the thought that it was all her imagination. To her mind, the teacher was just as much in love with her as she was with him. Because he never made any advances to her, she even went so far as to say that he must be so full of sexual inhibitions that he had a mental block. The fact of the matter was that the teacher was not attracted to her in this way, but she refused to believe it.

The Life of the Imagination

The life of the imagination offers one possible means of accessing the deeper root of the problem in the MNH. As described in detail in the chapter on "Reincarnation and the Archetypes," use is made of an archetypal figure that helps to make the repressed material conscious by resonating with it. When, as the consultation proceeded, we allowed the connections we had identified to "ring a bell" in our minds and when we really studied the situation, we obtained mental images which she fully confirmed. Saturn on the 8th cusp seemed to us to be like a person in authority, the archetypal figure of the stern judge who upholds the fabric of society and its laws and had passed a verdict of guilty on "delinquent" Venus on the cusp of the 5th house. She felt sure that she had become a social outcast because of her single lapse, and she was very apprehensive of being punished and misjudged. On the other hand, she was also judging others in the same Saturnian mode, because the roles are always capable of being reversed in the Moon-Node horoscope. With this placement of Saturn, she is both the judge and the accused. Possibly, in an earlier incarnation, she had been a male judge who loaded the feminine and the erotically sexual with guilt feelings, denying and repressing them, or even treating them as infernal. With Saturn in the MNH, Saturn is always two-edged in everything: one side is just as true as the other, and the native has to take the positive with the negative.

The Thought-Axis 3/9

We went on to discuss the theme of the 3/9 Thought-Axis, along with which there is an opposition between Jupiter-Moon and Uranus-Mars in Anna's radix. I described her capacity for independent thought and her potential in striving for comprehension. Here was where a solution to her old problem lay, but she had to find it herself. In fact, on the occasion of her second visit two months later, she worked out that the whole affair had been a case of self-deception. She said that the first consultation had done her good, because she had been able to survey her problem from a higher viewpoint. She had been able to accept the horoscope as a neutral means of diagnosis. The opinions expressed by those who knew her, she had felt to be judgmental (Saturn in the 8th house in the MNH). She did say, however, that the knowledge had reached no further than her head, and that her heart was still aching.

The Solution

As already indicated, the first step toward a solution involves the Ascending Node in the 9th house and also involves Sagittarius, the sign on the Ascendant (which sets the aims of individual development). We discussed this theme very thoroughly. It is up to Anna to deal with her guilt feelings by using her own awareness, experience, and powers of discrimination. The great learning triangle (red-green-blue) helps her to assimilate, neutralize, and objectify what she perceives as a painful moral quandry. She will increasingly realize that her bad conscience comes from outside; either from some defunct authority, or from a fate that ran its course in the distant past and is no longer relevant. What matters today is to accept her femininity, by permitting her 5th-house Venus to experience physical love without guilt feelings. In this way she can slowly impress on her unconscious the fact that social mores have altered and that being a woman is something very beautiful. Thus she herself can correct her distorted image of femininity, with considerable help (as it happens) from the current climate of opinion.

What is more, in Aries, it is typical of Venus to be demanding; and when she is oppressed by guilt feelings through a square from Saturn, she will sometimes relieve the pressure explosively, will act on impulse, and will cease to bother about guilt feelings. Perhaps the native needs to give free rein to her feminine sexuality for a time, and to enjoy it with more abandon, in order to develop her own conscience and her own lifestyle. According to C.G. Jung's theory of individuation, what many should do is to take what has been denied them and to cast off old constraints so that they can come into their own. Certainly, in the example before us, Sagittarius on the AC encourages this approach, since it is a sign that rejects indoctrination and does not brook outside interference. As an individual sign, it concentrates on its own aims and values.

If Anna does not free herself, whe will fall into similar situations and become infatuated with other men who do not reciprocate her affection. She will repeat the same bitter experience until she has broken the vicious circle by her own creative thought (Uranus) and autonomous will (Pluto), and has undergone a change.

The Node in the 9th House

The Ascending Node has Uranus, Pluto and Mars as helpers in the 9th house, and this gives a powerful boost to the dynamics of development. Anna is a quick learner and will recognize that she can work at the formation of her personal standards and sense of right and wrong with the serious intention of heeding this inner authority. With Aquarius prominent, she becomes increasingly able to free herself of self-deception and intrusive guilt-feelings. She will develop realism as she throws off the obsolete ideas of the past and learns from modern psychology.

It will dawn on her that the "wild woman" in her is a creative force that she can use in her artistic career. She would like to

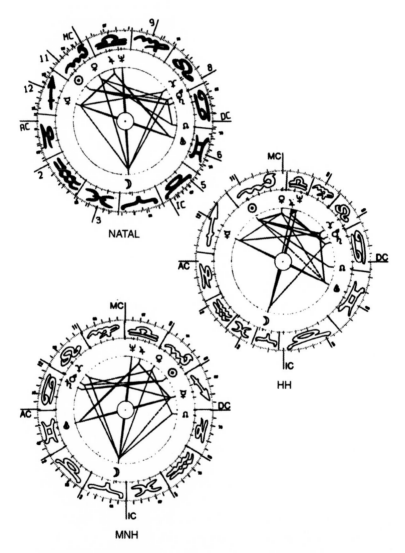

NATAL

HH

MNH

Chart 24. Elvira. November 16, 1945, 11:00, Burgdorf, Switzerland. Koch houses. Birth data from birth certificate.

become an art teacher; and indeed, the Sun in Gemini, the conjunction of the Moon and Jupiter on the 3rd cusp, plus the conjunction of Mars and Uranus near the 9th cusp, point to her ability to impart knowledge with originality and emotional insight.

Case #2: Anorexia as a Symptom of a Spiritual Crisis

Elvira has suffered from anorexia for many years. At the time of the consultation she weighed only 42 kilos (92.5 lbs). She had heard of out Institute and wanted to discover, through a consultation using the three horoscopes, the psychological background and spiritual correlations of her illness. She had been seen by several physicians and therapists, but with little benefit. Now she looked forward to receiving answers to her problems through an astrological approach. See Chart 24.

The Radix

In considering the radix, we do not think to begin with that she could suffer from anorexia. We see the physical "I," Saturn in Cancer with a relaxed trine to the Sun. (In the House Horoscope the trine has disappeared, and the Sun now has a square to Mars and Pluto and is therefore under tension.) On making a closer study of the situation, we establish that the Sun and Saturn each have unilateral aspects to Mars; they stand virtually aloof in the aspect-figure. The Moon, the juvenile emotional "I," is the tension ruler of the aspect figure in the fixed region of the 3rd house, and is in opposition to Neptune, which is "out on a limb." From the position of the Sun, Saturn, and the Moon, we infer that the family set-up was not what it should have been. This already gives us an indication: psychologically speaking, anorexia is a disease by means of which one tries to distance oneself from the role-models of the parents, and especially from the role-model of the mother if one is a girl or woman. The sufferers display an active, decisive, (auto-)

aggressive form of behavior; the mother is repudiated and "punished" for her conduct, and is made to suffer over the unhappy plight of her daughter. A readiness to react to emotional rejection by rejecting food can also be used against individuals other than the parents in a definitely subliminal way.

The House Horoscope

According to circumstances, the House Horoscope, too, supplies us with information. As already mentioned, Mars and Pluto are square to the Sun in this chart—an aspect pattern that usually indicates a problem with her father. In fact, there were times when the native hated her father and wished him dead. Whenever she disobeyed her mother, he used to say: "You will put your mother in her coffin." This rebuke was very hard to take, and it drove her to keep blaming herself. Since her "I" was already laden with guilt-feelings from former lives, these words had an adverse effect on her even though her father meant well.

The Age Point

To enable us to see the various correlations in more depth, we shall trace the growth of the problem with the Age Point. The trouble started at the early age of 4. There was an AP-opposition to Saturn, and she experienced repeated rejection by her mother, who had no time for her daughter's problems. And throughout her childhood she always felt she was being rejected. At the transit of the Moon when she was about 14, she had a hopeless crush on a teacher who, naturally, did not reciprocate her feelings. At the transit of Uranus when she was 31, the Age Point almost simultaneously made an opposition to Mercury on the 6/12 axis. During these months, she lost her entire former way of life. There was a total upheaval, she had to give up her occupation, she lost her position and her friends, nobody could or would help her, and her world fell apart. These terrible setbacks affected her physically; for the first time she fell seriously ill and eventually had to undergo an intestinal operation. An opposition on the 6/12 axis is typical of psychosomatic diseases.

At the transit of the Moon's Node when she was 53, she had recovered to some extent. At that time she secured a new job and had a new man-friend, who was, however, married. Once again, she was in a relationship with poor prospects. She thought that fate had thrown them together, and did everything she could to keep the affair going. She paid for the man's studies, gave up a great deal, and was very self-sacrificing, yet did not receive in return the satisfaction for which she craved. The hopelessness of the relationship gradually undermined the joy of life, and her one-sided devotion sapped her strength. She was no longer able to eat, her throat felt tight, and she fell ill again. At this time she began to think she might be better off dead.

Not only the Sun in Scorpio, but also Mars and Pluto foster thoughts of suicide. They cluster round the cusp of the 8th house and suggest some such drastic attempt to find a way out. Elvira tried to take her life on two occasions, but was unsuccessful. Therefore she could not and would not eat and became so emaciated that she seemed to be committing slow suicide.

The Moon-Node Horoscope

In order to obtain an even better understanding of the background of the case, we consulted the Moon-Node horoscope. There we see the Scorpio Sun in the 8th house, almost isolated, but with a trine to Saturn. The position of Saturn and Mars on the cusp of the 12th house makes us think of a former experience of isolation, probably in a cloister. The archetypal stimulus word "cloister life" produced an immediate reaction. In view of Elvira's suicidal tendency, it is safe to say that her "little me" had been pulled about by endless religious exercises and instead of gratifying her personal desires she had spent her time having ecstasies. The MNH as a whole points to such rarefied pursuits. Pluto in the

11th house and Neptune and Jupiter in the 9th, confirm that she has tried to sever worldly ties. She surmised, during the consultation, that she might have performed a priestly function in order to secure a place in heaven. (Unconsciously, Scorpio in the 8th house always looks for a reward of some kind.) It became clear to her that her self-sacrificing attitude and her willingness to forego the fulfilment of her wishes went hand in hand with the hope for a better life in the hereafter. Even as a child she had imagined what it would be like to live in a nunnery. She saw herself praying in the cloisters as part of a community.

We know that the experiences of former lives can have a residual effect in childhood; frequently, it turns out that what children want to be when they grow up is something they have already been in a former life.

Thus one can conclude, after studying the Moon-Node horoscope, that the medically diagnosed, neurotic suicidal tendency (anorexia nervosa), was present in former lives and may even have had a tragic outcome. It may be that psychiatric disorders (neuroses, psychoses) are involved, and that there are disturbed or bizarre forms of behavior carried over from many lives. However this may be, certainly it is true to say that a Scorpio Sun in the 8th house often points to a hidden suicide tendency.

The Placement of the Moon

The Moon, the emotional "I," intensifies faulty mental states, especially when it makes a tension aspect to Neptune. What is more, in the aspect picture here it is the tension ruler and therefore represents a painful point in Elvira's psyche. The opposition of the Moon to Neptune signifies unhappy love affairs in classical astrology, too. On comparing the two charts, we see that the Moon is in the 3rd house in both.

As already mentioned in the chapter on "Personality Planets in the Moon-Node Horoscope," there is no change when a planet occupies the same house in both charts (the radix and the Moon-Node horoscope). What this entailed in the case of Elvira was that she had been more than once confronted by the theme of self-deception in love (the opposition of the Moon to Neptune on the same axis). We can say in this instance that the transformation of the egocentric lunar desire into the universal principle of love represented by Neptune is an "old theme." The sole difference is the positioning within the house. The native has already done a lot of living in the compensatory mode of the opposition to Neptune, because in the MNH this opposition occurs in the stress region in front of the 4/10 axis. Long ago, in the cloister, it was usual to sublimate personal affections into a mystical state. She intended her urges to rise purified to God, like the phoenix from the ashes. The correspondences for this position are: a high love ideal, an inaccessible teacher, a friend who is already married.

Even in her present incarnation, she lived emotionally in the 3rd house: this time in the intercepted sign Aries on the 3/9 Thought Axis. Taking refuge in religion no longer works for her, and now she experiences defeats in her direct contacts because she finds it so hard to express her feelings. On the other hand, planets in intercepted signs are under cover, and the world around cannot get at them. Yet, in the 3rd house, the Moon remains dependent on the environment, is soon influenced and easily becomes the plaything of inner and outer images. She is as keen as ever to be thought of by others as friendly and charming; she is very accommodating, yet fails to obtain inner satisfaction. She makes herself emotionally dependent on the opinions and encouragement of others, but is not fulfilled. (When judging an "I"-planet in the same house—in this case the Moon—the reader is advised to remember the three stages described in the chapter on "Personality Planets in the Moon-Node Horoscope.")

In Elvira, the tendency to compensate is strong. For one thing, if mechanical habits are abandoned, will there be any hope of further self-development and stressless learning?

The Radix

Whenever there are deep problems, one should return to the study of the radix in order to activate self-healing forces. Consider the placement of the Sun in Elvira's radix. It stands on the cusp of the 11th house and has blue aspects. This means that Elvira should develop her sense of self-importance and should become more independent from her environment. In one of its facets, the 11th house is the environment, and has to do with independence from watching friends. She ought no longer to accept the evaluation of her father, her husband, and others, or allow herself to be discouraged by what they think of her. With this elevated Sun, she is elite, cultivated and refined; she is a person of worth and can make her presence felt. Helpful factors here, in addition to the Sun, are the Capricorn Ascendant and Venus on the MC; also Pluto in Leo with the talent triangle to the Moon and Mercury. This nucleus needs to be brought to life; which can be done by recognizing Pluto as the image of the "higher self," as her inner core.

At the time of the consultation, the Age Point was approaching Pluto. It is a period in which she is able to summon up the necessary self-assurance to discount what others think of her. For so long she has suffered under her dependence and has made herself ill while trying to hold her own against the ignorance or selfishness of those around her. Now she has joined a group-therapy class, where she has taken up art. She gets satisfaction from writing and painting. An inner self-healing power is already at work here and she must live in accordance with it, as it will help her to cross the Plutonic threshold. She must learn to say "Yes" to herself, and to accept her fate as something that is given to help her to mature.

Venus on the MC

Another interesting feature is the placement of Venus on the MC high in the zenith. Elvira belied her femininity in her long self-destructive phase. Incredibly, with this position of Venus, she had wanted to be a boy, had always worn pants and ties and felt ashamed of being a girl. In the House Horoscope, Venus has a small learning triangle to Mars and the Sun, thus there is quite a concerted action of animus and anima—as she learned at home. However, constellations in the House Horoscope are often experienced as "role-playing" and hinder a vital experience. Because of the different aspecting of Venus in the radix and the House Horoscope, the disguising of the anima as an animus is a not very helpful, though conceivable, solution. However, in such cases, compensations are always present, too. Here a part is played even by a tendency toward compensation carried over from former lives, in which sexuality was sublimated into piety.

Frequently, in Moon-Node horoscopes with marked indications of monasticism, self-conquest, and self-castigation, we also find a tendency to regard sexuality as dirty, and to repress or even denounce it as of the devil. This tendency is invariably accompanied by unconscious guilt-feelings. Elvira was affected in such a way that she could never give herself to her partner and experience herself as a woman. She kept having the same ideas of devotion that had already been exposed as self-deception at the Moon/Neptune-opposition.

Age Point: Transit of Pluto

As already said, Elvira's Age Point is now transiting Pluto. Previously, in the aspect hole between Mars and Pluto on the 8th cusp, she faced death; in a state of hopelessness she committed herself to the hospital with the idea of being helped to die. But the physician said, "She is not ill enough to die; she must regain the will to live."

Spiritually, Pluto is the nuclear energy, the pneuma, the core, the center of the being, in humans. When Pluto is transited, the inner core is activated, and usually this activation destroys the false ego-forms that do not belong to the essence of the individual's nature. This is the metamorphosis, the spiritual crisis, that occurs with each Pluto experience. Elvira, too, will face the metamorphic processes, and she is ready to do so, because she has sufficiently purified her body and her psyche, not only in former lives, but also in this life. Now the time has come to build up, to be renewed, to defeat the death-wish, in keeping with Elvira's Sun sign, Scorpio: "I am a warrior and a victor!"

Pluto will lead her to the gateway that opens either to death or to a new life. She will realize that, with Pluto, even her own will to live can be resuscitated. If she can honestly and consistently tell herself: "Yes, I want to live, I will no longer be ill," then regenerating Plutonic forces will be released, and the higher self to which she can now abandon her self, will become active and will take over her inner guidance. This process is known as self-initiation. In the long run nobody can help her but herself, as once more she takes the risk of placing confidence in life.

Epilogue

We received her report a month later. She had "made it." She had caught a glimpse of the threshold and was near to death, but at the height of the crisis, she came to herself. She realized the deeper meaning of this crisis of consciousness and suddenly knew that the development of her spiritual self had begun several incarnations ago. Her personal self had to learn to keep still and to allow itself to be cultivated by the spirit. This was something she could accept only when she knew "why." The three horoscopes together were decisive in helping her to help herself.

Concluding Thoughts

In spite of our positive experiences with Moon-Node astrology, there are no definitive answers to questions concerning the root of our being. No astrologer should imagine that he or she is an expert who knows the answer to every question; we must remain humble. Finally, one cannot be an astrologer without being genuinely religious. Whoever goes deeply and fundamentally into astrology as a universal concept of humanity and the cosmos, will understand the boundaries of the human spirit. Just beyond these boundaries there is the reality of God, that mighty Powe that is the source of our being. To this mighty Power we are all subordinate: "In Him we live, and move, and have our being."

Bibliography

Arroyo, Stephen. *Astrology, Karma and Transformation: The Inner Dimensions of the Birth Chart.* Sebastopol, CA: CRCS Publications.

Assagioli, Roberto. *Psychosynthesis: A Manual of Principles and Techniques.* New York: Penguin, 1971.

"Zeitschrift fur Astrologische Psychologie." *Astrolog.* Obertilistrasse 4, CH-8134 Adliswil: Redaktion, Jahrgange 1981–1991.

Atkinson, R. J. *Stonehenge.* London: Hamish Hamilton, 1956. Reprint: New York: Viking Penguin, 1992.

Bailey, Alice A. *A Treatise on Cosmic Fire.* New York: Lucis, 1951. Reprint: New York: Lucis, 1989.

———. *A Treatise on White Magic.* New York: Lucis, 1934. Reprint: New York: Lucis, 1991.

———. *Esoteric Astrology.* New York: Lucis, 1951.

———. *Esoteric Healing.* New York: Lucis, 1953.

———. *Esoteric Psychology.* New York: Lucis, 1962.

———. *The Rays and the Initiations.* New York: Lucis, 1960.

Blavatsky, Helena P. *The Secret Doctrine.* London: Theosophical Publishing House, 1893. Reprint: Wheaton, IL: Theosophical Publishing House, 1993.

Brunton, Paul. *The Quest of the Overself.* York Beach, ME: Samuel Weiser, 1970.

Dethlefsen, Thorwald. *Challenge of Fate.* Boston: Coventure, 1984.

Dürckheim, Karlfried G. *Vom doppelten Ursprung des Menschen.* Freiburg, Germany: Herder-Verlag, 1973.

Göbel, Dieter. *Das Abenteuer des Denkens.* Wiesbaden, Germany: Fourier Verlag, 1976.

Grof, Stanislav, and Christina Grof. *Spiritual Emergency.* Los Angeles: J. P. Tarcher, 1989.

Hawkins, Gerald S. *Beyond Stonehenge.* London: Arrow Books Ltd., 1973. Reprint: New York: Dorset Press, 1989.

Huber, Bruno. *Astrological Psychosynthesis.* London: The Aquarian Press, 1991. An American edition of this book will be published by Samuel Weiser, York Beach, Maine, in 1995.

Huber, Bruno and Louise Huber. *Astrology and the Spiritual Path.* York Beach, ME: Samuel Weiser, 1990.

————. *Lifeclock.* York Beach, ME: Samuel Weiser, 1994. This book was originally published in two volumes: *Lifeclock, Volume 1: Age Progression in the Horoscope.* York Beach, ME: Samuel Weiser, 1982; and *Lifeclock, Volume 2: Practical Techniques for Counseling Age Progression in the Horoscope.* York Beach, ME: Samuel Weiser, 1986. The revised edition includes an index.

————. *The Astrological Houses.* York Beach, ME: Samuel Weiser, 1978.

Huber, Louise. *Reflections & Meditations on the Signs of the Zodiac.* Tempe, AZ: American Federation of Astrologers, 1990.

————. *Was ist esoterische Astrologie?* Zurich, Switzerland: Astrologische-Psychologisches Institut, 1976.

Jung, C. G. "On the Psychology of the Unconscious" in *The Collected Works of C. G. Jung,* trans. R. F. C. Hull, Bollingen Series XX. Volume 7: *Two Essays on Analytical Psychology,* Princeton, NJ: Princeton University Press, 1953.

————. *Memories, Dreams, Reflections.* Edited by Aniela Jaffe. New York: Random House, 1965. Reprint: New York: Random House, 1989.

Neumann, Erich. *Ursprungsgeschichte des Bewusstseins.* Zurich, Switzerland: Rascher-Verlag, 1949.

Rudhyar, Dane. *The Astrology of Personality.* Santa Fe, NM: Aurora Press, 1991.

Index

in houses, 45
in Leo, 80
in Libra, 82
in Pisces, 86
in Sagittarius, 83
in Signs, 75
in Taurus, 77
in Virgo, 81
Radical Age Point, 114
Three House Sectors, 39
unaspected, 36
with Jupiter, 34
with Mars, 33
with Mercury, 32
with Moon, 30
with Neptune, 35
with Pluto, 36
with Saturn, 32
with Sun, 31
with Uranus, 34
with Venus, 33
mutable personality, 204

Nietzsche, Friedrich, 47
Nora, 197

opposition, 24, 25, 114, 185

peregrine planets, 183
personality planets, 191, 202
planets in same house, 179
possession axis, 118
power structures, 165, 186
prana, 131
psychological methods, 151

quineunx, 28

reincarnation, 139, 153
reincarnation archetypes, 155
reincarnation therapy, 140
relationship axis, 122
reminiscences, 154
reversal, 148
Rousseau, Henri, 67
Rudhyar, Dane, 12

sailor, 159
Saturn point, 15
secondary personalities, 184
semisextile, 28
sextile, 27
shadow, 145, 146
    integration, 150
social worker, 195
spiritual path, 129
square, 24, 26
Sri Aurobindo, 69
Steiner, Rudolf, 129
stimulus words, 158
Stonehenge, 7
stress sector, 42
Susanne, 189
synthesis, 149

Teilhard de Chardin, Pierre, 59
theory of relativity, 149
thought axis, 120
three-dimensionality, 179
three horoscopes, 105, 207, 210
    evolution in, 111
triggers, 157
trine, 27

universal soul, 131

For over thirty years Louise and Bruno Huber have been working with astrological psychology—teaching, training, and writing. They are the founders of the internationally recognized Astrological Psychology Institute (API) in Adliswil/Zürich, Switzerland, and the English Huber School in Devon, England. In addition to personal counseling practices, the Hubers teach at both schools, and lecture all over the world. They have been keynote speakers at the American Federation of Astrologers Convention and since 1981 they have been co-organizers of the now-famous International World Congress in Astrology held every year in Lucerne, Switzerland. They are the authors of several books including *Astrology and The Spiritual Path, Lifeclock: The Huber Method of Timing in the Horoscope* and *The Astrological Houses.*